Grace Slick

Grace Slick

THE BIOGRAPHY

Barbara Rowes

1980
DOUBLEDAY & COMPANY, INC.
GARDEN CITY, NEW YORK

For the Memory of
Scott Kaleko

ISBN: 0-385-13390-1
Library of Congress Catalog Card Number 78–22351

ACKNOWLEDGMENTS

On July 6, 1977, I flew into San Francisco with tape recorder and suitcase full of yellow legal pads. Jefferson Starship sent a chauffeured limousine to pick me up. The driver dropped me on Van Ness at the Holiday Inn. It was the wrong hotel. Two hours later, I arrived at 2400 Fulton Street for the first interview. Grace did not show up. "I had developed a stomach virus. I was at home," she later explained, "throwing up."

Books do not spring to life. They evolve through experiences. This biography grew at a slow and erratic pace through two years of research and writing. The idea was born through a natural rapport which developed between Jean Bennent Cummings, who was an editor at Doubleday, and myself. Over a lunch I suggested a biography of Grace Slick, whom I had studied for an article in the New York *Times* on July 4, 1976. That following spring Grace and her manager Bill Thompson flew into New York City to confirm plans with Doubleday. The following week attorneys Bob Gordon on the West Coast and Jeremy Nussbaum on the East Coast commenced negotiations. The contract was signed soon thereafter.

Without RCA Records this project could not have been completed. They proved silent patrons of inspiration and good friends to an often harassed and frantic writer. Stu Ginsburg originally introduced me to the Starship for a cover story in *Scholastic Magazine.* Throughout the gestation of the book, even after he left RCA for Atlantic Records, he was a motivating spirit. When times got rough, Herb Helman was always there for me with a substantial dose of trust and confidence. Mel Ilberman offered any assistance and trusted me with his insights.

I want to give special acknowledgment to Marguerite Renz, assistant to Herb Helman, who is single-handedly responsible for at least a third of the listings and statistics from which I was able to draw. She was not only responsive and attentive, she radiated kindness and honesty.

Much of the research in these pages was drawn from the memories and impressions of people who gave hours upon hours to recollect often painful and difficult things. The number of people who gave me interviews is too large to list individually. However, these few people listened freely, offered encouragement and gave a great deal of time to me. With affection and great appreciation to:

Virginia and Ivan Wing, who always made me feel like part of their family. Their trust touched me.

Jerry Slick, who did everything possible to help me find facts. He is a kind and generous spirit.

Spencer Dryden, whose mind is a history of rock in San Francisco during the 1960s and whose soul is pure gold.

Finally I want to offer these personal recognitions. No writer gets through a book alone. There are always friends who fill her with confidence, warmth and the knowledge of her experiences. To these very special people in my life I offer deep appreciation:

Carolyn Reiff, who has long been a muse of courage in my life teaching me to work instead of wallow.

Walter Ong, who has been a source of inspiration since my first day at New York University.

James Michener, who took time to teach me about publishing and life.

Bob Gordon, who believed in me as a writer before I believed in myself.

Martin Bernheimer, Richard Stolley and Campbell Geeslin, who brought me up as a journalist and taught me the importance of caring about every fact and innuendo.

Carol Guardino and Joanna Krotz, for their friendship.

and

Grace Slick for two years of confidences, trust and an unfinished and rare friendship between two very different women. Thank you, Grouser.

Barbara Rowes, 1979

1

In the early hours when dawn filters sunlight through the San Francisco fog, Maid Marian wanders inconspicuously through Haight-Ashbury, then disappears into the forest of Golden Gate Park. It is the Summer of Love, 1967.

Standing on the corner of Haight Street observing her is an unemployed flautist named Roddy, an unofficial herald of the dawn playing the airs of Vivaldi. Rainbows of graffiti form a psychedelic backdrop behind him on a tenement wall. To his left three willowy, if not malnourished, nymphs are dancing to his sylvan notes with miniature bells around their ankles, fingers and noses. On the pavement beneath their feet are the words of Timothy Leary—"turn on, tune in, drop out"—gracefully being trampled under their toes. A few blocks down on Cole Street a combination of grocery and headshop is already open. In the window hangs a sign warning local patrons: "Do Not Take Thorazine, Seconal and Downers for STP Bum Trips. If you need help, call Free Medical Clinic. 431-1714, 588 Clay Street." A pair of love beads hangs underneath it, still unclaimed after three days.

For months the neighborhood has been overflowing with transient drug freaks, tourists and runaways settling for a night or two in crash pads. A barefoot soul sister named Joanie has been raising her crystalline soprano in fragile Child Ballads on Cole Street like a pureblood alley cat. Her soulmate Bobby has been mumbling his tone poems on Stanyan Avenue, stoned on the roaches of old marijuana cigarettes thrown into his tin pan. Two days ago, Joanie and Bobby disappeared from their respective street stages, their origins unknown, their destinations unchartered.

In the early glow of this morning, as the sun is rising, the streets are blossoming with grinning flower children. Thousands have been streaming in from all over the country to settle in Haight-Ashbury and live according to the gospel of Timothy Leary. It is a modern pilgrimage of the 1960s: a crusade of free spirits; a liberation of the love generation dropping out of the straight society to create their own life-styles.

At noon a love-in is scheduled on the Polo Grounds of Golden Gate Park. The event has drawn an even greater population to the area and created a crisis for its volunteer agencies. The Housing Office, which rarely opens, is now working overtime to screen runaways and find crash pads for vagabonds. The Medical Clinic, which treats hippies free of charge a couple of hours a week, is now besieged with emergency calls since two teenyboppers died on June 14 of overdoses in Golden Gate Park. Bread lines have formed in front of the Free Store on Cole Street where the Diggers, the local underground salvation army, provide free food and clothing to the hungry and threadbare.

For nearly five years Haight-Ashbury had grown and survived as an inner city sanctum of off-the-wall radicalism. What flourished in its midst was unbridled hedonism: a free flow of drugs and instant love where the only values were to have fun and feel good. It was a cartoon reality without the political rhetoric of its beatnik forefathers: a nomadic tribe of existentialists who played life as a comedy of errors unharassed by the police since it posed no threat to the establishment, at least at first: a freak show of uninhibited creative instincts with animated soundtrack by the Beatles and backdrops by Andy Warhol where experiences unfolded as a daily happening.

As long as it retained the innocence of Wonderland, Haight-Ashbury remained the original theater of the absurd: a street ensemble which changed nightly. On Tuesday an unemployed journalist named Tommy put on his black mask and galloped through the streets as the Lone Ranger. Sam the Record Man was the starring attraction on Thursday when he donned his helmet as Sir Lancelot and charged through Cole Street in search of his Guinevere.

On June 22 at 4:45 A.M., a dark-haired lady of mystery made her entrance on the scene as Maid Marian. Swathed in a medieval cape and large shades, she wore a suede skirt and vest, black peasant blouse with bodice tightly reined and high buccaneer boots to hide her chunky knees. She strolled the streets as a silent spectator of the living scenario.

"Gracie?" one of the threadbare flower children called after her. She turned, smiled and vanished into Sherwood Forest.

2

Ten days before the delivery, Virginia Barnett Wing had a sudden premonition about the character of her child. Not prone to superstition, she dismissed it from her mind and mentioned it only in passing to her husband.

On the morning of Halloween Eve, October 30, 1939, she was awakened by an unusual sensation. Her husband Ivan reassured her that each birth had its peculiar omens; but her premonitions grew stronger with every contraction. By 7:37 A.M. her two-hour labor ended in the birth of her daughter Grace Barnett Wing: a seven-pound cherub with a devilish glint in her clouded eyes. The attending physician had never seen an infant so unruffled by the trauma of birth; Grace was quite unwrinkled upon making her debut into the world.

Rebellion and self-confidence characterized Grace's spirit, which, even in infancy, had unusual intensity. After the first few years, Virginia threw out her child care books. Grace was not conforming to the usual behavior patterns: childhood was proving just a fast passing phase in her development, and by the age of three she had already dispensed with the preliminaries. While other children were crayoning in coloring books, she was sketching surrealistic renditions of the masterpieces in her father's art history books. A year afterward, she started listening to her mother's semi-classical recordings, then choreographing dances to them. On her fourth birthday, as a finale to the *"Peer Gynt* Suite," she climbed up on the piano and plunked out her own interpretation of Grieg's melodies—perhaps not exactly what Ed-

vard had had in mind in terms of notes, but at least the spirit
was there.

Her mother took this living portrait of a young artist in her
stride: musicians had long run in her family. Grace's great-
grandmother Lizzie Whitman, an Annie Oakley type, was the
first pioneer to carry violin and guitar on the wagon train into
the Northwest Territory, a one-woman orchestra on the new
frontier. In the 1880s she was even awarded a headdress by the
Lapland Indians for teaching English folk songs on their reserva-
tion. At the turn of the century, when she had grown weary of
her geographically limited repertoire, she grabbed her son
Marcus, Grace's grandfather, and left her husband in Lewiston,
Idaho, to attend the concert season in the nation's capital.
Marcus Barnett was subsequently raised in the orchestra seats of
the leading concert halls. There he developed an inordinate love
of classical music and expressed it through his lyric tenor. He
passed his voice on to his youngest daughter Virginia in the next
generation. After graduating from the University of Washington,
where she bumped into Ivan Wing prophetically in a music
class, Virginia pursued a singing career in Hollywood but retired
prematurely to marry Ivan, who was an investment banker.

Grace fell heir to this exalted tradition but proved less singer
and musician than living symphony. Music revolved through her
mind in a continuous soundtrack; there were times when Virginia found her in the dark silence of her bedroom staring into
space with her foot tapping to the quick rhythms of her mind.
When she called this peculiar behavior to the attention of her
husband, Ivan advised her not to fret about it. Grace seemed
able to take care of herself. The two of them consequently took a
back seat to Grace's artistic development and watched as their
living symphony began to play in society.

In 1943 Ivan was transferred out of Chicago and the Wings
moved to San Francisco. Ivan was moving up the ladder of the
investment banking world in Weeden and Company. Grace
enrolled in public school and there faced her first confrontation
with the establishment. The rigid system proved inflexible and

unsympathetic to the free spirit who choreographed "Åse's
Death" and danced draped in a white sheet à la Isadora Duncan
on the bare floor of the cloakroom. For that, she was banished
from the class and reprimanded by the principal.

Her schoolwork suffered from similar improvisations. Her es-
says tinted the heroes of the American Revolution with the dramatic foibles of Red Ryder. Her contempt for arithmetic was legendary by the fourth grade when she devised her own system of
multiplication which was instantly canceled out by the principal.
Her compositions were pure poetry and consequently difficult to
read.

By the time the Wings moved to the affluent suburb of Palo
Alto, where Grace's brother Chris was born in 1948, she was set
in her patterns of merely acceptable scholarship. When the class
was one place, Grace's mind was someplace else; she simply
didn't "apply" herself to the business at hand. As a result, her
grades suffered and her mother grew distressed as she watched
Grace slowly withdraw from reality to live in a self-protective
fantasy world. In the late afternoons Grace would disappear into
the vacant lot behind the schoolyard, transforming the piles of
junk into a Sherwood Forest of the mind. There she would in-
habit the fractured landscape with the adventures of Robin
Hood, naturally casting herself as beautiful Maid Marian. When
her mother came to get her, she would find Grace curled up
under a tree lost in her own reveries.

All children live in their own world, but Grace's imagination
was positively overpopulated with castles, knights, ballerinas,
glass slippers and Mad Hatters who did not fade away with increasing maturity. "When the other kids would play with baby
dolls or jump rope, I would go off alone to live through my fantasies." By the age of eight, she was hanging out in the museums
comparing the ambers of Rembrandt with the flesh tones of Ti-
tian. "I had my closest relationships with the dead painters, but I
couldn't talk about serious art with the other kids because they
weren't into it as I was and they would make fun of me for liking
it." She became a closet intellectual while her social personality
became a self-made caricature of a stand-up comic or enter-

taining con man; a cultivated identity to hide her own vulnerability and creativity. Typically and unfortunately, she overcompensated for her sensitivity and ended up with hard-edged sarcasm.

Around the fifth grade her teacher called in her mother to complain that Grace was metamorphosing from a high intellect into a smart aleck. Though she attracted attention by becoming class jester through her visionary bravado, "I had the feeling that the only time people ever liked me was when I was funny and performing." After school in the playground she would entertain her classmates with her tall tales. Her grandmother was such a master of ice skating and she traveled so speedily that no one could see her; consequently she only skated at night with lights on her clothes so people could catch at least a glimmer of the performance. Grace herself was the long lost daughter of Superman, given up for adoption by Wonder Woman, waiting for just the right moment to reveal her superpowers. When all the kids on her block were riding their bikes forward, Grace would deliberately be the one on the handlebars pedaling backward. Since she was always traveling in the opposite direction from the crowd she had many acquaintances but no close friends. She drew her constant companions from the characters in Grimm's fairy tales, and for a while she became Amy in *Little Women* "because she was the prettiest sister who wanted to become an artist," but she later metamorphosed into Alice in Wonderland "because she had better adventures."

For a long time Grace's parents nurtured her creativity when in the evenings she reprinted the pictures in her books into a vital reality. In the midst of their cocktail hour, she would suddenly appear as entertainment on center stage in the living room, where she performed in self-designed costumes as Maid Marian, Mozart or Alice, depending on her particular program. There she would express her inner visions and share her companions in fantasy. Her father gave her rave reviews for this show of ingenuity and even rushed for his camera to take her picture for his photograph album. Thus Grace developed her performances into a living room repertoire. "We didn't have a TV yet and my parents would be sitting there going blind reading all the time, so all of this was a welcome diversion for them. I didn't do it all the time but I did do it often enough. When I let this out in front of my parents I got rewarded for it, whereas with kids my own age it was a different thing altogether. I always had dozens of different people I could become whenever I wanted to, while the other kids were always the same. They were always predictable, while I never seemed to know what I was going to do next."

Grace's next move was a typical one for an adolescent. Whatever pursuits she had had which had once set her apart were now set aside in favor of those which would make her popular. Out of the closet came her new leather jacket, saddle shoes, cheerleading pompons and even a little early R&B to replace the classical records she had put into mothballs. Her mother, who had been a straight A student in convent school, was not thrilled by this sudden conversion, but Grace was no longer seeking her approval. She was hungry for acceptance by her peers. To score points with the "in" crowd, she stole cigarettes for them, guzzled liquor straight out of the bottle and even surreptitiously "borrowed" the family car to illegally drive her friends around during her sleepover parties. Despite her rites of initiation she was unanimously rejected by them on her fourteenth birthday when twenty of the hottest young ladies phoned to say they could not stand her. Grace was shattered, feeling she had lost every friend in the world.

Though Grace was devastated by this rejection, her mother was secretly relieved. For some time Virginia had been encouraging Grace to transfer out of Palo Alto High School into Castilleja School for Girls, a local finishing school which would provide rehabilitation in the social graces. Grace had long been at odds with her mother about her social breeding. She was naturally rebellious against the unwritten but nevertheless restrictive codes of proper conduct. But Virginia came from a long line of blue bloods. Her ancestry in this country dated back to John Whitman, a Puritan who had left England to settle Weymouth, Massachusetts, in 1638. Over the next three centuries her forebears managed to reserve their place in history as, somewhat ironically, the leading architects of the American establishment. Her most famous relative was John Cabell Breckinridge, who was Vice-President of the United States and then ran for President against Abraham Lincoln before dropping out of the Union to serve as Secretary of War in the Confederacy.

Grace was the product of the family's rebel strain. Her ancestors in the nineteenth century were the leading pioneers and missionaries of the American Northwest Territory. Her own maternal grandmother, Susan Barnett, was an infamous libertarian raised by a straitlaced political father who was an Idaho state legislator with heavy connections in Washington. In 1917 Grandma dropped out of straight society when she left her husband for another man. Divorce in her high circles was, according to Grace, about "as usual as running down the street with your clothes off." Nevertheless Lady Sue, as Grace called her as a child, followed her free spirit and resettled in Seattle, Washington, with her beau. There she brewed beer in her basement during Prohibition and circulated it among her friends in the underground of the 1920s.

Though Grace had a natural rapport with her free-style grandma, by the age of fifteen her relations with her more conventional mother were strained. "At that time—and maybe all the time always because it's just as true now as it was then—the blonde with big boobs was *it*. That was what the men wanted, and that's what the media gave to them as the ideal woman. And my mother fit the bill perfectly, and I didn't. My mother was prettier, warmer, smarter than anybody else's and she had a beautiful sexy figure, while I was built more like my father."

Natural though this mother/daughter rivalry was, it did nothing to enforce Grace's self-image as a woman. On Christmas Eve, 1956, Grace's unconscious fears were realized in a minor incident. Joe McCarthy (not *the* Joe McCarthy) had been her boyfriend for nearly two years when he had abruptly broken up with her not long before, "turning me over for one of those big-boobed blondes." Grace was shattered by his rejection and moped around the house for months hoping he would call her again. That Christmas Eve he showed up at her door unexpectedly and handed her a present. Thrilled, she ran to her room to open it. When she ripped open the card, she saw the gift was for her mother.

Virginia was unaware of her daughter's feelings of inferiority since she took great pride in Grace's creative talents and recognized her free spirit as a chip off the old block of Lady Sue. As a strict disciplinarian and perfectionist, though, she was always after Grace to get on the right track and improve herself "because I just knew that she was not living up to her potential." What she did not fully comprehend were Grace's feelings of defeat before she had even entered the competition. "No matter how well I ever did, I did not feel I could ever win."

By the time she first enrolled at Castilleja in September 1955, Grace was drinking heavily: screwdrivers on the green lawns of the finishing school where the headmistress thought she was drinking orange juice; later in the evening straight gin out of the bottle she stole from her parents' liquor cabinet. Nobody, including Grace, fully realized the depth of her problem. Her parents dismissed her drinking as a rite of passage. Her friends thought it was a symptom of her wild rebellion. Grace herself did not question the unquenchable thirst since it relieved the nagging question of her own self-worth haunting her mind as graduation approached.

With poor grades and low self-esteem, Grace had not surprisingly harbored no grand ambitions about going to college. Nevertheless, she enrolled at Finch College near Park Avenue in New York, then a breeding ground for rich co-eds to graduate *summa cum laude* with husbands from the Ivy League. "I wanted to see New York and I knew I could not get into Columbia." She was a loner at Finch, falling back on her creative resources and finding companionship in the melancholy folk songs of Odetta which she played on her guitar in her bedroom. Though she made an instant connection with Celeste Shane, a Beverly Hills socialite who had been kicked out of eight prep schools and was expelled from Finch in November, she was different from the other girls there only to find husbands. Grace in 1957 was still looking for herself. She explored New York with the refreshing naïveté of a Neil Simon heroine: eating hamburgers at P. J. Clarke's, running barefoot through the snow in Central Park. On weekends, the script was straight J. D. Salinger, when she took the train to Princeton for rendezvous with her steady boyfriend, a kindred spirit who was president of Princeton's drinking club. Grace made an impression on the Princeton campus in the winter of 1958 when she was chosen as a pinup girl of the Tiger Club and photographed for their newsletter. Despite her social accomplishment and the opportunity to marry a hard-drinking thoroughbred, Grace was bored by the pretensions of the Ivy League. In her sophomore year she transferred to the University of Miami, then a notorious party school, where she majored in art.

When Grace flew back to Palo Alto in the spring of 1959, she had reached a turning point. "If Picasso had enrolled in my art classes, they probably would have given him a C." When she was able to do in classes what she wanted, there was no problem, but she had no patience with the basic liberal arts system. "For an artist to grow there must be free natural expression, and that wasn't what the universities were offering."

In September 1959, Grace Wing exchanged the educational system for the business world. For the next nine months she pursued her fortunes through the classified ads in the San Francisco *Chronicle:* a two-day stint at the switchboard for a law office where she quit after her boss reprimanded her for talking back to his biggest client; an audition for a recording contract with a new record label for which she sang "It Ain't Necessarily So" for four black honchos who were not exactly looking for a token white; finally, an interview with an ad agency which ripped off her ideas for Bank of America.

In July 1960, she received an unexpected phone call from Celeste Shane (who was eventually to marry film director John Huston), asking her to come down to Beverly Hills and help her organize the Kennedy Girls for the presidential campaign. Grace spent the summer hobnobbing with Celeste and her girl friend, actress Jill St. John. Together they attended political parties where Pierre Salinger cast her an eye, "but I still never registered to vote because I did not believe in the political system."

When she returned to Palo Alto in September, she had made up her mind to become a fashion model in San Francisco. "I already had a lot of experience in the field since I had been posing for my father's camera since I was three years old." Celeste and Jill told her to forget it: she didn't have the body. Even her parents waxed skeptical. Grace followed her own instinct, however, enrolled at the House of Charm and five months later appeared as a cover girl in a bathing suit for the Sunday magazine of the San Francisco *Chronicle*.

She had finally made it in the land of big-boobed blondes, but her social life was in a slump. Her mother reintroduced her to her neighbor Jerry Slick (the handsome son of Virginia's best friend Betty), who like Grace had been a prep school rebel and had just finished doing penance in the United States Army. Grace attracted his attention by doing her high-powered imitation of Lauren Bacall. She blew smoke in his face, and straddled the kitchen chair backward. It had taken Jerry two weeks to learn the Morse code in the Army; Grace bet him she could learn it completely in a single night.

Jerry was fascinated by the girl-next-door playacting as a worldly woman. She had turned him on with her sarcastic remarks and impenetrable glacial come-on. On the next day, as promised, she stopped by his house. Though it may sound unbelievable, she actually had mastered the entire Morse code in a night. "Grace is too much for him," Virginia worried aloud, but oddly enough Jerry wasn't intimidated. He was interested.

The romance bloomed over the next few weeks as a companionship of convenience. At twenty-one, Jerry was an insecure, straight preppie who was still looking for his niche as a freshman at Foothill Junior College. Grace was a free spirit in search of the right rebellion. Together they shared a contempt for bourgeois values and an ambition to escape from suburbia. A month after they first held hands, Grace asked him to marry her. "I really just wanted to live with him but it would have killed my mother."

In Grace, Jerry found the strength and challenge he was still lacking. In Jerry, Grace saw a husband who would win the approval of her mother. Unpredictably skeptical about this union, Virginia remained silent and planned an elegant wedding. Ivan Wing had by then been made a vice-president of his firm Weeden and Company and become prominent enough in the field to earn honorable mention in Who's Who in America. As a result of his status, the wedding on August 26, 1961, was no small social event that summer season in suburbia. The ceremony was appropriately staged at Grace Cathedral in San Francisco with the reception in the Gold Room of the Fairmont Hotel. The bride and groom flew off for a first-class honeymoon in Hawaii, then moved into a small apartment in San Diego, where Jerry had transferred into the State University.

Grace worked in the accounting office of a leading department store and hung out with Jerry's relatives, loyal John Birchers who recruited the newlyweds for marches to stop the spread of communism. As the days passed, the couple's communication became stricter and minimal. Both had been loners throughout their lives and "we had strong walls built around our emotions." In the evenings, Jerry studied and Grace withdrew into her shell to express her feelings through the folk songs of Joan Baez and the Kingston Trio. "Living with Grace was like being married to a long-playing album. Music was part of the decor of the living room." Her guitar playing was an inspired soundtrack in an otherwise prosaic reality. Though Jerry was stimulated by his classes in school, Grace was quietly going nuts. For all its beauty, San Diego was not a cultural community, and despite her resistance, Grace was first and foremost an intellectual. Starved for bookshops, museums and the cultural ambience of San Francisco, she began expressing her discontent in letters to her parents "Jerry got good grades at the Institution," she wrote them on November 1. "Me learning how to cook after a fashion, also cleaning toilets, sink, etc. One hundred and seven degrees in the shade here, no air conditioner in our palace, not even good for breathing. My grocer who was from New York originally hates this place with a passion only a New Yorker could feel. The only friend we have here is our landlady but that doesn't count. We pay her to be friendly. I got the nerve to ask my grocer how come he is here if he hates it so much. He says you don't got to be crazy to move here but you gotta be crazy to stay."

In response to her urging, Jerry put in an application to San Francisco State College, which was the intellectual center of the cultural renaissance taking place in northern California. In December he was accepted. Grace enthusiastically packed their belongings and moved out of their suburban life-style into the burgeoning counterculture of the 1960s in San Francisco.

3

One can't walk very far on the streets of San Francisco; you'll kill yourself trying to get three feet ahead because you have to walk ten feet straight up to do it. Never one for much in the way of exercise, Grace still would go out once in a while early in the morning to walk her cat. The white Persian, Walt, would play on his end of the clothesline leash while Grace took in the sights on hers. The Slicks were now living in the Potrero Hill section of the city, a neighborhood which had at one time been an enclave of Russian immigrants. The section had evolved from its ethnic origins through a blue-collar period into a reasonably inexpensive area for artists and students, its streets trafficked by Volkswagens, bicycles and motorcycles.

The Slicks' little white house had seen better days. Their landlady, who lived next door, had survived a prolonged stay in a Nazi concentration camp, which had instilled in her an extreme paranoia about anyone in uniform. She kept watch over her property with a loaded shotgun, and one probably apocryphal story has it that she had once unexpectedly opened fire and narrowly missed killing a Good Humor man.

Though there were definite drawbacks to this outpost on Kansas Street—what it lacked in paint it made up for in mice—the rent, $95 a month, was irresistible. In a way this move was Grace's unofficial declaration of independence from the values of her parents, who were predictably "concerned" by their child's sudden downward mobility. When Ivan first saw two Hell's Angels revving up across the street, he even offered to subsidize a change of address himself. But Grace was immovable. It was her life, and she was going to live it herself.

Jerry was now full-swing into a film study career at San Francisco State. Having shot his first movie months earlier, he had decided to become a cinematographer. Grace meanwhile was pursuing her own intellectual career sans curriculum. Her world view was becoming heavily influenced by Gibbon's *Decline and Fall of the Roman Empire,* from which she developed a cyclical theory of history and politics. "Somebody has the power and somebody else doesn't. The power at the top can't hold forever, and as time goes by the little people get more and more of the power themselves one way or the other until they are actually the ones in charge themselves." The hypothesis held as well for the minor movements of transient national politics as it did for the major movements of revolutions, dynasties and empires. "It didn't matter to me who got elected to what, or which radical group was trying to take over from which establishment power. Sooner or later the positions would be reversed, so there wasn't much point in getting too excited about any of it."

Some of this political nonchalance can probably be traced back to her own middle-class origins, but in a way this attitude informed much of the politics of the sixties. The "youth movement" which rallied around the anti-Vietnam War synecdoche may have been directed by political activists, but its vastest numbers were simply middle-class kids who didn't want their asses blown off in some Southeast Asian jungle. When the war died, the movement died with it, but the actual political system remained essentially unchanged. Even the activists were eventually absorbed out of the mainstream. Few followed even remotely political careers.

"This isn't to say that I didn't have strong feelings about what was going on around me, or if some son of a bitch got elected and screwed everybody up against a wall it didn't mean anything to me." In fact, Grace was quite vocal about her Gibbon-oriented political thinking. She enjoyed talking it out, thinking about it, exchanging ideas, working it out as she went along. She even tried her ideas on Ivan during one of their infrequent family get-togethers, but Ivan merely thought his daughter's ideas were silly. "I guess you couldn't really expect him to break down in the middle of a discussion, smitten by my impeccable arguments, and admit that he'd been wrong all these years."

As a corollary to Grace's political theories, she developed at this time a strong aversion to money and material wealth. In contrast to the trappings of her continuing career as a high-fashion model at Magnin's, she was slowly unloading much of her own wardrobe at the Salvation Army. Additionally, she had sold off most of their wedding gifts, including some fairly valuable crystal and silver items. "The problem with money and things is that you've got to watch out for them. If you've got silver you've got to polish the shit. If you've got two pairs of shoes you can only wear one but you've got to keep track of the other pair at the same time. If you take money and invest it you've got to watch it or hire somebody else to watch it. I prefer ideas to things; I just don't like too much 'stuff.' What I'd get rid of were things I had no use for, like six matching highball glasses. What the hell could I do with six matching highball glasses? I didn't have six matching friends to go with them."

Eventually, at around the time of the assassination of John Kennedy, she quit Magnin's and settled down as an unemployed housewife, spending a lot of time listening to records, accompanying herself on the guitar. She had the habit of playing the same groove on an album over and over again, "until I became it and it stuck in my brain, and probably drove Jerry crazy at the same time." The major hymns of the season were the songs of Bob Dylan: disgruntled poems with visions of hypocrisy and low-key grumblings of disillusionment. Dylan explored guilt and rebellion in Hamlet-like soliloquies which pricked the conscience of the new age through the newfound air waves of FM radio then growing in popularity. Grace was gripped by the raw truths of Dylan, who moved through the spirit of her generation like a pied piper. The undercurrents of the growing counterculture were just beginning to percolate in San Francisco, through the graffiti on the walls and the writing in the pamphlets being handed out on the streets. Grungy-looking pot-smoking orators preached loudly on the corners, crying heroically: "I don't own a tie or suit" or "I am an orphan of America" or "Nobody ever starved in the streets of Berkeley."

On some afternoons, with Walt scampering at her feet, Grace would follow these freaks to get the news out of the mouths of the rebels about the latest student demonstration on campus or a bust of the Oakland motorcycle police, "who belonged behind bars themselves." Despite her currency on the scene, she never stopped in People's Park to picnic on soybeans or enlist in the Free Speech Movement. "Why should I join a society for freedom," she asked herself, "when I was born liberated? The problem resides in the system, not in me. It's the politicians who ought to be the activists in SDS."

Beneath her rhetoric was her stonewall resistance to making a complete commitment to the radical ideology. "I am a real chicken," she confessed to her husband, "but if I had the guts I'd drift out of this society straight into the seventh dimension." Ironically, two weeks later, it was he, not she, who made the connection with the underground. The hookup happened one morning on the ⌗43 Roosevelt bus traveling uphill to school when Jerry, by design of the fates, sat down next to Roy Baxter. The quiet-spoken black bureaucrat, who procured automatic-fire electronic parts for the government by day, was a notorious budget gourmet after dark. His position in the kitchen was unrivaled in San Francisco, where no galloping gourmet could hold a fork to Baxter's red-hot skillet. Neither Julia Child nor James Beard had mastered, or even attempted, the production of an "instant" chocolate soufflé. Neither Melina Mercouri nor Aristotle Onassis had ever snacked on macrobiotic stuffed grape leaves. Not even Colonel Sanders had finger-licked *organic* chicken crispened on a solar barbeque. Not only was Baxter a premier chef, he was also a first-rate patron of the avant-garde, who gathered every Saturday at his apartment on Mount Olympus, an ancient but heavenly residential district in the Twin Peaks area of the city.

Jerry was unaware of the notorious reputation of his busmate. The two rode side by side through three stops in silence, then transferred together. While waiting for a ⌗45 bus on Market

Street, they struck up a conversation, reviewing the news of the day in topical chitchat which got surprisingly heavy when Jerry introduced the headline story about the ex-hog-cutter Antonio De Angelis, just arrested for the greatest swindle in history: a record $175 million in profit for substituting seawater for salad oil. When Baxter heard the news, he went bananas, for the swindle threatened to jeopardize the high quality of his salads. Jerry tried to soothe his disquieted spirit and finally succeeded in calming him down by changing the subject to film. As he described his latest idea for a project, an existential comedy about the conditions of paradox, Baxter sensed Jerry's potential as a member of the avant-garde. Figuring he would fit in with his crowd, he invited him to the Bacchanal on Mount Olympus on the following Saturday night.

Grace was thrilled when she heard. For months the Slicks had been discreetly banned from the *de rigeuer* rent parties held throughout North Beach where the hosts charged a dollar or so for admission to their open house; in fact, Grace's and Jerry's names were even dropped from potluck dinner lists. "What's wrong with *them* for not inviting us?" she would ask Jerry. "What's their hang-up?" Jerry did not bother to correct her perspective. Why burst the bubble of such a healthy ego? But he was well aware of how Grace's now fairly heavy "social" drinking affected the heads of other people. "If I were you," cracked one observer, "I'd lease my wife out to the Viet Cong. She's the first guerrilla fighter who ever attacked me head-on at a cocktail party."

At these functions Grace changed into another person—the kind of alter ego nobody wants to become too well acquainted with; in fact, she wasn't even the kind of person she wanted to know, "but there wasn't much I could do about that," she confessed, "because my brains got all screwed up on alcohol. I just have the feeling that there are two different women living inside of me." Despite this admission, she never got the two of them together, "because I was never on both sides of my personality at once." The "other" Grace essentially only arose at parties where "I was afraid nobody would want to talk to the real me."

The fear stemmed back to the long-lost hours of her childhood when she sneaked down the steps to watch the adults socializing at the parties of her parents. During these critical spying expeditions, she saw dull, inert neighbors—"the mothers and fathers of my friends"—becoming perfectly charming, if not utterly fascinating, characters. Her usually quiet father sparkled with congeniality and her smart-looking mother turned into a very foxy lady. Wide-eyed and mesmerized by the transformations in their behavior, Grace was deeply impressed by the adventure of socializing, "but I didn't think I could ever be really good at it since I was too reserved and frightened of saying the wrong thing and being rejected at these kinds of social gatherings."

Though Grace was always ebullient upon receiving an invitation to a party, her underlying fear of being the only oddball in the room began to erupt the moment she walked in the door. Before she even looked around at the other people, she was hitting the bottle to transform herself into another person who could cope with her competitive desire to hold the major spotlight on the scene.

Jerry, who had watched her act again and again, would withdraw solemnly to the other side of the room "to keep out of her line of fire." From afar he would watch his wife turn into Elizabeth Taylor out of Albee's *Virginia Woolf*. Without deliberate or conscious malice she would attack the most vulnerable creatures around, preferably men, whom she would argue into the ground for her own mental recreation. According to Jerry, "she should have been a prosecuting attorney."

As a result of the conventions of the 1950s, which dictated the housewife role to girls of her generation, Grace exercised her talent for *argumentum ad hominem* at parties, which presented her only forum for lengthy debates. It was hard to pigeonhole her tactics for provoking unsuspecting guests into opponents in a contest of iron wills, but generally she nailed any guy whose vulnerability she could quickly identify and attacked him about it with a sudden lashing of her tongue. Her victims often fled to the other side of the room, but Grace, who loved an artful scrimmage, would follow them and lay verbal siege again.

These episodes, to her, were one way of cutting through the chitchat which "put me to sleep." She never recognized the cruelty of her verbal assaults or their effect on her unsuspecting victims, nor was she aware of her growing reputation. What concerned her most, in a blindness to the situation, was her failure to stab anybody who would strike back. "When I put the ball into play I wanted to find somebody who could return it."

The more Grace argued, the more Jerry turned off to her; by the early winter months of 1964, he had even begun occasionally philandering—while Grace remained as faithful as Penelope. One evening as a party was drawing to an uneventful ending, she could not find Jerry to take her home. Still high and antagonistic from her verbal slaughter of a half-crocked podiatrist, she grabbed her coat and walked the two miles to Kansas Street on her own. When she reached the house, she saw the car and figured Jerry had come back early—but apparently not to be alone. There on the couch, drinking *her* cold duck, were Jerry and a ravishing brunette who had taken off her spike heels—and black stockings.

"Kind of lonely walking home alone," Grace remarked as she pattered by them and closed the door of the bedroom. Half an hour later, after dropping off his friend, Jerry came home ready for an all-out confrontation. Instead, he entered a dim-lit house. The lights in the bedroom were all turned off and Grace was sleeping peacefully on her side of their double bed. "She never even mentioned it," he said incredulously. "Why should I?" she replied to his inquiry several days later. "I figured the two of you were obviously enjoying each other so why change it."

Unnerved by her blind faith and unfathomable—if not frankly unbelievable—nonchalance, Jerry increased the distance between them by becoming totally absorbed in filmmaking; by the winter of 1964, the marriage had reached a standstill.

The parties at Baxter's attracted a wide cross section of characters. Here was a chance to exchange sober ideas with all manner of people and, for both Grace and Jerry, it was an entree into a world where others were willing to accept them on their own terms. Whatever it was that was going on in San Francisco, the Slicks were now a part of it. They became Saturday night regulars at Baxter's free-form soirees.

Grace had recently turned on to Lenny Bruce, and she was repeating the Adolf Hitler routine from his first album at Baxter's one evening when she was interrupted by a debonair Britisher who grabbed her left breast in his own variation on the more conventional handshake. True to her own sense of cool, Grace went right on talking—while he went right on pawing her. "This guy was from another planet," she cracked afterward; "still, there is something refreshing about a finely warped sense of humor."

Gordon Lassar, a chemist, was an early import from England, a mod type who had been successful in the construction industry. Grace was impressed by Lassar's versatility with a test tube. By day he wore a suit and tie as a leading chemist of industry; by night he pored over his books, like a medieval alchemist, a Merlin, looking for the best recipes for ways of expanding the dimensions of the human mind.

Through his constant exploration of mind expansion—a prodigious ingestion of the popular experiences of Aldous Huxley, Timothy Leary and Alan Watts—the quiet-spoken Englishman had developed into a scholar of hallucinogens. In the evenings, even Jerry would cut short his filmmaking to listen to Lassar talk about the new frontiers in mind expansion. Like the very drugs he was discussing—mescaline and LSD—he turned on their consciousness to a new dimension of experience and the "ultimate adventure and challenge of seeing things differently from previous generations." Scared but thrilled by the dare of experimentation, Grace nevertheless lay back long after the others had gone ahead, "because I did not want to screw up my head," but gradually she came forward through the tutelage of Gordon, who wisely appealed to her sense of reasoning. Highlighting pertinent passages from *The Doors of Perception,* he asked her whether she thought taking drugs would be any worse for her than smoking cigarettes or drinking alcohol. After thinking about it and getting a confirmation from the printed word of Huxley, she had to agree. "The only reason I take alcohol rather than hallucinogens," she surmised in conclusion, "is probably because some corrupt politician got a kickback for making the stuff legal. 'All the vegetable sedatives and narcotics,'" she read from Huxley, "'all the euphorics that grow on trees, the hallucinogens that ripen in berries . . . all . . . have been used by human beings from times immemorial.'"

Gordon had purchased some fresh peyote buttons from a mail-order operation in Laredo, Texas. In April he invited the Slicks with two other couples to his flat, where he stewed up the peyote with vinegar and water until it was concentrated into thick, brown juice. Grace was still apprehensive about attending this psychedelic tea party, but gained courage from the realization that "my first experience was under the supervision of a leading chemist—just as Huxley had first taken mescaline in 1953 under medical direction."

Still nervous, she tried to make amusing small talk to lessen her own anxiety but Gordon was straight scientific business and requested reverential silence like a priest measuring out holy water. In the kitchen he filled shot glasses full of the liquid—and provided lemon juice as a chaser to be drunk immediately after to stop them from vomiting from the putrid taste of the hallucinogen.

Grace followed the procedure but felt no kick from the stuff for forty-five minutes after drinking it. "I don't think hallucinogens work on me," she confided to Gordon, who was still hanging out in the kitchen. Gradually she drifted out into the back yard. Five minutes later, she saw herself slowly opening into the next level of consciousness. "In the right setting this is a beautiful evolution of the intuitive cycle. A lot of people have tried to explain it, but the entrance of an individual into realities that are guided predominantly by the spirit is a wordless phenomenon that can only be experienced. The conditions of the high exist on levels that are beyond the rational systems that we have come to worship as being the 'final word.' What hallucinogens show you is that there *is* no final word. The journey is endless and our present thought forms haven't even scratched the surface."

4

After parties at Baxter's Saturday night Grace would return unannounced on Sunday mornings. Without saying a word, she'd walk over to the sink and start scrubbing his finest china—with a fresh can of Ajax and scouring pads. Baxter was touched by these extemporaneous cleanup campaigns, but surprised and taken aback by Grace's sudden appearances at his doorstep. But Grace felt a certain responsibility to do her share since she and Jerry had become regulars at Baxter's. It was the least she could do—and it certainly was better than having all those parties at *her* place.

Eventually Baxter grew to expect Grace's Sunday arrivals. Once the place was pretty much in shape, she would stretch out on the floor and begin to rap with him about the friends they had in common. It was a run-on tête-à-tête with Baxter interrupting her monologue to throw in his recipes for instant potato chip dips. Grace was intense and insatiable in her curiosity about the backgrounds of the characters at the parties; Baxter kept her up-to-date through his natural talent for gossiping, and well fed through his unbelievable generosity with leftovers. She did not, however, care for his current choice of music, John, Paul, George and Ringo. For several months she had wondered "Why these guys?" through their hit singles: their choirboy demeanor made her feel as if she was "eating two pounds of bonbons. Those guys were so sweet that listening to them gave me a stomachache—even if they did have ten gold records this season. The very title 'Mop Tops' suggests a 'Look how cute I am' appeal that sounds like it's aimed at somebody's grandmother."

At the source of her criticism was her own sense of injustice about the irrelevance of their lyrics. "While my generation was getting high on 'I Saw Her Standing There,' nineteen Panamanians and four U.S. students bled to death during the riots at the university. In the midst of the greatest sexual revolution this side of the Garden of Eden, can you believe that their biggest song in this country was still 'I Want to Hold Your Hand'?"

Baxter understood her exaggerated concern and tried to encourage her to stop picking on the Beatles and get in there to compose some relevant music on her own. He had often heard her improvising on her guitar and singing during his parties, but at this time the idea of being a professional musician was not one she took seriously.

For several months, Jerry had been working long days into nights on his senior thesis—an existential comedy of errors which his good friend Bill Piersol had scripted into a movie. Though without linear plot, the madcap string of episodes came up with surprising depth in its comic renditions on the absurdity of the human condition—where, according to Grace, "a freak for peace could go home from an anti-war demonstration and beat up his wife" or "a judge who was a closet alcoholic could try a normally sober person for drunken driving." Jerry had shot the footage by day, watching the rushes in a studio at San Francisco State College by night (Grace herself played several different but essentially anonymous roles).

The film was to be titled *Everybody Hits Their Brother Once*. Before it would be complete it would need background music for the soundtrack, and Grace just naturally fell into the writing of that music. Jerry taught her how to use multiple recording tracks to solve the problem of her lack of musical training. Instead of writing down music for other people to follow, she played the music herself, one track at a time, layering the instruments on top of each other until the songs developed the way she originally conceived them.

Jerry and Grace worked nights at the music studio at San Francisco State, Jerry on control board, Grace on guitar, piano and recorder. The music simply "came out." The introductory theme for the film was an intricate three-track composition which was eventually to be recorded as "Jay," in honor of Jerry, on her solo album *Manhole*.

"When she first heard herself singing counterpoint with her own voice and playing against herself on the guitar, she couldn't believe it," Jerry said, "but after a while she began to get pretty cocky about it." At a party soon afterward he heard her telling Baxter that she might have become a "one-woman chamber orchestra, except there isn't much of a market in it . . . yet."

The film won first prize at the Ann Arbor Film Festival. As a result, it went on tour to the other festivals in this country and abroad, establishing Jerry Slick as one of the leading young cinematographers in northern California. By June 1964 he had graduated out of the classroom and was going on locations for professional shoots. As his reputation grew, he was spending less and less time at home. Grace once asked to go along with him, but he turned her down without a second thought.

This was a time in San Francisco when it was a simple matter to move from one apartment to another whenever one happened to feel like it, and Grace usually felt like it more often than not. She was never one to become very much attached to places or things, and "once you decided you didn't like your house any more there was bound to be another place." Their next move took them to a white stucco cottage in the high rent suburb of Tiburon, where Grace developed a new friendship with Jerry's brother Darby, recently returned from a stint in the army. With Jerry away for recurrent stretches of a day or two working on his films, Darby gradually became Grace's most constant companion. Darby was a student of things mystical and Indian, which he shared with Grace. She began introducing him to the new ways of San Francisco and things Western, casually winning him over with her own recipes for toasted marijuana seeds, which she'd salt and wrap in tinfoil and pop into a 500° oven for around a minute before serving to him as an hors d'oeuvre.

There in the living room, against the background of the new British rock which was invading the scene, they began to create their own musical harmonies. Darby was the superior guitarman, according to Grace, "because he could play specific tunes as they were written," while she, untutored in the basic chords, "could only improvise and play *around* the songs." As a result, Darby played the original melodies of pop songs with Grace weaving in and out of their tonal lines with her light skirmishes on guitar and vocal improvisations reinterpreting the structures of the music.

That there was more going on between his wife and his brother than just music was obvious to Jerry, who was well aware of what turns their marriage was taking through his own extracurricular activities. In many ways it was an extension of a time and place rather than a personal situation. There was so much happening—people coming and going, experimentation with drugs, the first rush of the reborn rock of the sixties—that their loose marriage seemed to fit in quite acceptably. Although not articulated as such, it was an early example of the sexual freedom which was soon to become a manifesto of the generation.

Drug trips became a frequent pastime within the ever widening circle of San Francisco musicians and artists and just plain folks who would eventually be given the sobriquet "hippies." The Slicks were by now regulars on the scene, taking in sunrises on the hills of Mill Valley and sunsets on boat rides on the Bay, and whatever else in between. Grace was among the heartiest experimenters. If 50 milligrams of acid were phenomenal, 100 would be twice as phenomenal, 200 four times as phenomenal, in a geometric progression into deep space which left some of her companions, including Jerry, dumbfounded. Whatever the intoxicant, Grace always seemed to do it with more fervor than anyone else. Ostensibly, it was "to see what would happen," and few people tried to stop her from following her own path to the heights.

Continually moving on the psychedelic front, the Slicks continued moving on the home front as well. One morning a notice appeared on the bathroom mirror:

> Due to Circumstances Beyond My Control
> We are Moving to Larkspur Next Wed.
>
> > Sincerely,
> > Grace Slick

It was a white wooden house in another rural suburb with the quintessential doper's bathroom: two medicine cabinets, one labeled hard drugs, the other soft drugs, "one for recreational purposes, the other for medicinal routines. I was always afraid of getting the mouthwash mixed up with the mescaline or taking tablets of aspirin instead of acid. Hell, that could be dangerous: too much aspirin can be fatal!" On a ledge beside the john she kept the *Physician's Desk Reference* as a handy guide "to stop yourself from blowing your brains away."

Meanwhile the living room was collecting its own paraphernalia—guitars, piano, Jerry's drums he had once played, Grace's recorder—in a scene being mirrored in other houses around the area. Nearby North Beach had long been known as a West Coast haven for displaced eastern jazz musicians. In the seedy backstreet clubs the improvisations of Charlie Parker, Lester Young, Thelonious Monk and Roland Kirk had created a Jazz Age in the 1950s which eventually yielded its dominant impulse to the poetry of the beats in 1958. Now, seven years later, around the garrets and Victorian houses of Haight-Ashbury, a strange metamorphosis in beat poetry was beginning to be heard: it was an instant conversion of the poetic meter into a more intensive electronic beat, the birth of a new American rock idiom within Grace's own listening range.

Among the first friends Grace made among performing rock musicians were the Charlatans, one of the only groups with a reputation outside of San Francisco (specifically Virginia City, Nevada, which was in fact no small achievement for a local group at that time). They played loose rehearsals together in a Victorian house in Haight-Ashbury, and because of their growing professional status Grace was a little in awe of these five long-haired characters who looked like cattle rustlers out of a grade B Western. Hanging out with the Charlatans were members of another group already playing around the area whose physical appearance made the rustlers of the Charlatans look like Sunday school teachers. Originally known, appropriately enough, as the Warlocks, they would eventually be known as the Grateful Dead, their individuality in both life-style and music putting them at the vanguard of American music.

The variations on the San Francisco let's-start-a-rock-band theme developed into a heavy growth of second-rate instrumentalists, most of them dropouts from the folk music circuit. There were usually four to six guys who played instruments, "and a tone-deaf seventh who, for lack of anything better to do, became their manager." Most of the groups to surface out of this climate of experimentation were eventually to disappear without a trace, but others, like the Dead, the Jefferson Airplane and, in Sausalito, playing in a houseboat on San Francisco Bay, Quicksilver Messenger Service, were slowly beginning to play local clubs, building both their talents and their followings.

Accompanying the music was yet another area of new ideas, the visual. Architect George Hunter, a part-time member of the Charlatans, was a prime mover on this front. As a graphic artist, his perceptions of rock were originally translated onto the wall of the Red Dog Saloon in Virginia City, Nevada, as the first official light show in the summer of 1965. Hunter's offbeat collages and paintings began appearing on the walls of local clubs, and were the forerunners of the soon-to-blossom psychedelic art posters.

While Jerry spent most of his energies making and watching films, Grace kept track of all the local musicians. "Living with Grace in those months was like having a direct line to Wolfman Jack. The only thing she could talk about was the bands and their different styles of music and presentation. Finally I gave her the *Chronicle* one morning and asked her to refocus on race riots or the starving children in Africa."

It was in the *Chronicle* that Grace spotted a photograph of rock musician Marty Balin (who she assumed was a Filipino), opening at a new club called the Matrix with his group, the Jefferson Airplane. Since she had heard very little about them (the band would eventually become famous for its insularity), she was naturally eager to fill in the gap in her knowledge. She convinced Jerry to go with her to see them a week after they had first opened there on August 13, 1965.

The Matrix was down by the Bay on Fillmore Street in an off-the-beaten-track neighborhood called the Marina. Partly owned by the Jefferson Airplane, the club room was small and stuffy, the walls covered with psychedelic sketches of the musicians, graffiti paintings and a broad semblance of an airplane which "did not look as if it had enough power to stand on the ground, much less take off." On stage were five guys in street clothes and a female vocalist in pigtails and leather boots who had all the verve of a Giselle MacKenzie, but who sang with a rich rock contralto.

When their set was over, Grace had come to a resolution: she wanted to form her own rock and roll band. "If those guys could do it, we could do it." There was therefore no difficulty in Darby convincing Grace to seriously consider forming a group, but Jerry remained reluctant to put down his camera to pick up drumsticks. For over a year he had been building his reputation as a cinematographer: why should he give it up to become a musician?

From a purely economic point of view a career in rock for most was a mere pipe dream, but both Jerry and Darby were bolstered by a trust fund from their grandfather and could afford to indulge in whimsical ambitions. In the end, Jerry's agreement to join the group was essentially a move by him to remain a part of the excitement going on around him. While the film world was going every bit as crazy (if not more so) than the budding rock scene, there was no film community yet as such in San Francisco (unlike Southern California, which was just beginning to bring forth its Coppolas and Lukases). In a situation of either join up or miss out, Jerry joined up.

Thus the Slicks inaugurated their own nice little family band, and began cutting their teeth doing renditions of popular songs written by others. The group was a difficult creation from the beginning, destined never to live much past its first birthday. For barely thirteen months it struggled on the verge of making it but died suddenly in October 1966 when its mother abandoned it by running off with Jefferson Airplane; yet for its brief life-span, a fleeting tune-up in the great soundtrack of rock, it had an unrealized dramatic influence over the expanding strains of American rock; in fact, the Great Society contained the germinal spark of the artistic instinct which was to raise rock in this country to the very brink of the fine arts.

It was September when the gestation got formally under way, a sequence of small events which, according to Grace, developed a "logical progression to doing for profit what we used to do for fun—from sitting around singing folk songs to standing around playing rock and roll. The only difference was in the position." Friends hung out with them over the next few weeks and brought along their own guitars and bass for jams. For a while it looked like Jeanie Piersol, the wife of Jerry's best friend Bill, might have stuck around to beat the tambourine and harmonize with Grace but after a couple of rehearsals she stopped showing up. "I guess she couldn't stand listening to us," Grace quipped. "To play with us at that time you either had to hate music or love dope."

Though several friends of Darby and Jerry hung out with them, few guys ever stuck around. "We were just grateful if *anybody* came back." David Minor began jamming with them regularly and ended up singing and becoming the rhythm guitarist. Bard Du Pont was the bass player, and Peter Van Gelder, a saxophone player who was attending classes at the Ali Akbar College of Indian Music with Darby, was the last to join up, adding a touch of jazz to the party.

The casual rhythmic contractions of the early days intensified into regular three-to-four-hour rehearsals starting around 11 A.M. "As far as being good," Grace reflected, "we were not. Nobody knew how to play. We'd do what we called jam—but the only guy who could hold his instrument right side up was Peter Van Gelder. I thought the whole idea of forming a band was pretty funny since none of us were trained musicians, but then I figured if somebody was going to pay us, this bunch of goons, to get on the stage, who was I to blow it by pointing out how bad we were?" The official baptism took place in September with the christening of the group as the Great Society—a visual pun on Lyndon Johnson's political program.

Now all that remained to achieve professionalism was the problem of composing their own repertoire—a major undertaking, especially considering that none of them, except Grace, had ever written any music. But, "If guys like McCartney and

Lennon could compose a bunch of gold records, we could probably put together *one*."

In the next few days, modern literature was reborn. The musicians began showing up with streams of lyrics, metaphors and similes of their poetic spirits accompanied by the simple strumming of their guitar strings. Bard Du Pont was the most prolific of the lot, "and we were all very impressed with his productivity," Grace recalled tactfully, "but none of us could stand listening to his lyrics." They strongly suggested that he stick to his bass playing but Du Pont could not control his creative urges once unleashed. Eventually, when none of his songs ever went back for a replay, he faded out of the band. Jerry was similarly not cut out of the poet's mold; in fact, he was so cynical in his romantic outbursts that he made Dylan sound like the eternal optimist. Unlike Du Pont, Jerry stuck to the drums and the business matters (though he briefly hired John Carpenter at 10 per cent for manager), realizing that his greatest contribution to the group's survival was in *not* writing songs.

It was Darby who became their poet laureate. One night after a conversation with his girl friend on the phone, he started pouring out an upbeat love song called "Somebody to Love," and the next morning "the lyrics just flowed." It was a spiritual communion with the tempos of the Beatles' "I Want to Hold Your Hand" ingrained with a strange depth of cynicism in the lyrics. Grace creased the standard chords of his AM rock song with her offbeat resonance and winding improvisations through which she imitated the sound of the guitar with her voice. Ironically, it never occurred to her to get involved in the actual songwriting since "I heard rhythms, not lyrics, in my brains." Instead she cheered on the other musicians to unknown heights in songwriting by serving them her new specialty of frozen fishsticks with a unique recipe for tartar sauce which, according to Jerry, "included anything which happened to get underneath her fingernails."

Had fate—in the guise of Jerry—not intervened, Grace Slick might have gone down in rock history only for her recipes and singing, but her husband sort of pushed her into songwriting. "I finally locked her in the bedroom and told her not to come out until she had started composing."

Behind closed doors with guitar, piano, bass fiddle and a couple of joints, she scribbled lyrics on an empty page in her black spiral notebook. An hour later, she emerged with "White Rabbit." Jerry was knocked out by the song, which was nothing short of a literary classic in the genre of rock. Through the haunting pulsations of drum and piano she echoed the beats of Ravel's "Bolero," drawing Lewis Carroll's heroine as a rich archetype for her generation. "I didn't write *Alice in Wonderland*," she said later. "I only pointed out its relevance to my own generation: this whole creative flow is like putting my mind on automatic play."

"Since my first song was #1 with this band, there is nowhere to go with the sequel but downhill." On the contrary, her second contribution, a high-toned reverential upbeat for Lenny Bruce entitled "Father Bruce," was another smash hit in the living room.

Things had changed. The process of creating was arduous for her and aggravating for her husband. For days she would lock herself in their bedroom, where "she would throw away what could have been four or even five different types of songs before coming up with one she thought was right and good enough for us to play. The inefficiency of the process always killed me because she'd throw away better stuff than most people write down in an entire lifetime!" Jerry said. "She'd start off with a phrase, develop it and crumple it up. After a day the floor of our bedroom looked like a garbage dump inhabited by a mad poet. 'Listen, Grace,' I'd break in, 'you're only writing a second-rate song for a third-rate group—not the fifth novel for the *Alexandria Quartet.*'"

Still, she kept on rewriting until the songs had evolved into what she wanted them to be. When she finally handed in her last creation, the band had seven or eight songs ripe for performance "and so we sat around trying to figure out the right ordering. None of us had any idea what we were doing," she said, "but we knew we didn't have to call in Einstein to figure it out. It was basically a matter of common sense. I mean, you don't start off with a dirge unless you want to put the audience to sleep. And you try to begin with a familiar tune, which was rough at that time since nobody had even heard of us!"

By September 15, in his column in the San Francisco *Chronicle,* Ralph Gleason, the venerable Dean of Music in San Francisco, had published the official birth announcement for acid rock. "All over the country," he wrote, "young people are declaring themselves more interested in a career with a guitar than in getting their teeth capped, their noses straightened and trying out for a bit part in a Hollywood flick. It's part of the changing values of the society." Grace read the column, then scotch-taped it to Jerry's pillow. "I guess our generation," she scribbled in the margin, "has finally caught up with us."

A week later, the Great Society officially slipped into the vanguard through their first gig on Grant Avenue in North Beach at the Coffee Gallery. For years the old beatnik hangout had been sliding into decline. The neighborhood was once alive with poetry readings and coffeehouses but was now becoming populated with Chinese laundries and topless nightclubs. Though the Byrds had recently brought the area up-to-date with their performance of their "Mr. Tambourine Man" repertoire in the Peppermint Tree, none of the San Francisco bands had played this nightclub circuit yet.

The group survived its one-night-stand debut in a minor folk club. Jerry decided that success was on its way. In the *Chronicle* he had seen a notice for auditions for a contract with Autumn Records—a new company presided over by the "Big Daddy" of KYA radio, Tom Donahue, who, ahead of the times, was already on the FM wavelength. A businessman of flaky sensibility who always had a "piece" of the music scene around, he had recently invested in a topless nightclub in North Beach which was going downhill quickly. As a result, Donahue was looking to branch out into the greening fields of the then on-key flower children. On Saturdays in North Beach, he held auditions for the local bands, but the musicians tuning up were not yet old enough to walk into a club let alone sign a recording contract—in fact, Grace pointed out, "I doubt if any of those kids had even graduated from high school yet." At the age of twenty-six, ten years younger than Donahue, Grace felt like the oldest musician in the room. "In this crowd one thing was for sure: the Great Society stood out, if not by virtue of their music, then by virtue of their years."

Grace slipped out of the audition room into the bathroom with just enough alcohol to blot out the pimpled faces and loosen up her mounting anxiety. But when it was Great Society's turn to audition for the contract, she was still nervous. As she stepped onto the stage, she glanced at Jerry for reassurance, but he was fiddling behind her with his drumsticks. She looked sideways at Darby, but he was too busy tuning up his strings to notice her anxiety. Finally she swallowed her own fear and trembling and faced the Falstaffian figure of Donahue, then waiting to make the final judgment on her.

Her nerves were now revved up through jitters into a hyperactive energy. Behind her, she heard Darby's guitar strings taking off and Jerry's downbeat coming in for a quick landing. Gripping the microphone with all the force of her interior anxiety, she belted out the lyrics. A few minutes later, when the final guitar chords subsided, she was left standing there, still gripping the microphone, eyes closed, awaiting the verdict.

Donahue was totally unimpressed by the band—although it far outplayed the competition of the day—yet he was totally blown away by the corporeal alchemy of Grace Slick in her sweater, boots and mini-skirt, which were then *de rigueur* on the scene. "I figured he was just kinky enough to get turned on by my wide knees." From the beginning there were conflicts because Donahue "wanted us to do a more middle-of-the-road kind of rock"—he envisioned them opening his psychedelic rock club (now called Mother's) with Grace singing an upbeat version of "Summertime" with which the older generation could also connect. He pushed the group to work up a fast-tempo arrangement of Peter, Paul and Mary's hit single, "Leaving on a Jet Plane." When they appeared reluctant, he gave them "stacks of stuff—demos and tapes—to listen to," anything to get them more into the commercial mainstream where the money was then piling up.

But money was anathema to the musicians in the Great Society, who "only wanted to have fun and do their own thing." Grace confided to her friend Jeanie, "We figure we have to pull in enough to find someplace to live and eat well, but that is no big negotiation. Jerry can handle that. This is no fireball industry like movies. Rock music is just fun—it's laissez-faire creativity—just a bunch of goons like us fooling around with our instruments. Somebody ought to explain to Donahue that there's just no big money in this kind of thing."

Despite the pressure to become more commercial, the image of Great Society never underwent change. Though well-heeled rich rebels in fact, they saw themselves through romantic self-impressions as outlaws and bad guys—the West Coast replicas of the Rolling Stones—with Grace playing the leading role. The concept was dynamite, the reality less so. Though spiritual progenitors of acid rock, they were, in fact, "still a garage band," according to writer Ben Fong-Torres, then free-floating on the scene. "When I watched one of their performances, I always had the feeling that they were just tuning up."

There was, in fact, little professionalism around them. The Jefferson Airplane was playing Thursday to Sunday at the Matrix, where between eighty and a hundred people occasionally paid a buck to listen to folk lyrics recycled through the rhythms of rock. The Charlatans were top bananas visually but their days on the scene were numbered, as were their major gigs. Still, Grace had a special affinity with them because "they were so screwy you just couldn't help wondering how they ever put their shoes and socks on." She continued to drop by their Victorian mansion decorated by one of their old ladies named Lucy who had a florid imagination and a sense of interior decorating which might have appealed to Mel Brooks. "It was like a goddam museum," Grace recalls, "and I should have taken pictures of it as the prime example of a San Francisco hippie building: old brass beds with funny hanging lamps and big decorative old shades with funny fans and weird statues. I don't know where she got that stuff or whether or not she stole it because they sure didn't have any money."

Though the *Chronicle* was daily trumpeting the coming apoc-
alypse of sound through the columns of Gleason, Herb Caen
(who coined the term "hippies") and John Wasserman (with the
persistent probing of Bill Thompson, an enthusiastic copy boy
and roommate of Marty Balin who was functioning as a promotion man for the band), the high notes were actually few
and far between. When the Great Society opened at Mother's in
October, "the tables," according to Grace, "were virtually empty.
We were lucky if two or three drunks showed up." For the most
part the musicians played in the psychedelic club five sets six
nights a week, "a half an hour of music with a vodka and tonic
for the break," then checked out the bathrooms, where Donahue
had painted psychedelic murals on the walls. He had conceived
Mother's as a "giant womb" for the broad revolution incubating
in the arts. The walls were filled with unknown masterpieces of
modern art. In his final and desperate extension of this artistic
experimentation, he even hired Del Close to compose light shows
on the walls.

Despite his innovations, the Great Society failed to attract an
audience and sealed the doom of Mother's—and the final days of
North Beach as a creative nexus in the city. Though the band
did not succeed in building a following in the fall of 1965, it did
garner an unexpected laurel wreath from Ralph Gleason, who
roused interest in them and established their credibility when he
wrote that they were a band to watch and singled out Grace's
"Father Bruce" as a strong indication of the rising IQ in rock.
After the appearance of his review, local musicians started listening in. Different guys from Quicksilver Messenger hung out at
their gigs and even some of the Jefferson Airplane came around.

Though the Great Society bombed financially at Mother's,
Donahue was savvy enough to keep investing in their potential.
He even booked them into the Golden Gate Studios to make a
demo tape with ace producer Sylvester Stewart—alias Sly Stone.

There is no denying that Grace was nervous, especially when
she glimpsed Sly's Jaguar arrogantly parked in front of the fire
hydrant near the studio. As she walked through the door trailing
after Jerry and Darby, her fingers were trembling because before

her in the control room was sitting Mr. Cool himself and his tight friend, wild keyboardist Billy Preston.

As legend goes at that time, Sly was the Wizard of Oz behind the control board of the recording scene: an infamous musician who combined the artistry of Vladimir Horowitz, Miles Davis and Eric Clapton in his pinkie. He could, in fact, play any instrument and indeed was a one-man symphony. "This guy is never going to be able to stomach our playing," Grace whispered to Jerry.

There was indeed a gap in their musicianship and Sly made them uncomfortably aware of it, tolerating their session only because he was being paid for it. They were to make a demo of ten songs—with special attention to Darby's "Somebody to Love" and his Indian raga entitled "Free Advice," which were slated for release as their first single.

For a while the musicians loosened up but Sly broke their confidence when he couldn't help laughing at them "because we were so bad. For the most part we'd get started on a song but blow it halfway through by making some stupid mistake." When they obviously couldn't get it together, Sly suggested hiring some studio musicians to dub a couple of parts but this was the height of insult and the Great Society vetoed the stand-ins.

Though none of the session went particularly well, their recording of "Free Advice" has become legendary among the engineers and producers in the Bay area. "The first take of the song was pretty good," Jerry recalls, "but the engineer didn't get it. After that we just kept making mistakes, one after the other, so that Sly had to make them redo it 137 times"—undoubtedly some kind of warped record.

5

During the second week of October of 1965 a weird-looking fourteen-year-old in granny dress and wire-rim glasses tacked up a poster on a wall of Enrico's Coffee House on Broadway: an advertisement for the inauguration of rock and roll in San Francisco down in the longshoreman's Hall at Fisherman's Wharf. There the first and leading bands on the scene—Jefferson Airplane, the Charlatans, the Marbles (who were destined to vanish without a trace) and the Great Society—were heralding the new wave of sound in a dance for thousands of budding flower children. Over the next few months, the bands played on and the plots slowly thickened.

Behind the scenes of the Avalon Ballroom, California Hall, Carousal and the Fillmore, as well as the out-of-the-way Matrix, Grace continued her writing in the little black notebooks she constantly carried with her. In them were both rough and polished versions of lyrics (most of them never used), well-drawn sketches of characters real and imagined, and all the detritus of this scene of which she was an integral part.

Grace's major complaint, apology and explanation of the state-of-the-art rock scene was that its predominant characteristic was volume. "Rock music is totally distinctive," she explained to her parents, who deliberately steered clear of her concerts after hearing her description of them. "The lyrics are concerned with more than just the burned heartstrings of melodramatic lovers. When you boil down jazz it's basically the syncopation of rhythms, but rock is the first electronic music: it heightens the improvisations of jazz through the amplification of its instruments. I'd say the best rock singer would have to have the musical instincts of a vocalist like Ella Fitzgerald and the volume capabilities of an Ethel Merman."

Grace's own voice was an instrument of unusual resonance: a hidden breath of magical intensity and passionate depth which poured out of the gut and head in equal proportions. She was not really the only woman on the scene, of course; besides her, Signe Toly Anderson was belting out the background harmonies in flight with the Airplane, Lynne Hughes, an anachronistic fifties lady, occasionally got it on with the Charlatans, and Janis Joplin by then was up and coming out of Texas; but it was Grace who in 1965 was the recognizable soulmate of the acid scene. "It was not only how she sang," recalled the *Examiner's* music critic Phil Elwood, "but also how she looked." Half icon, half flesh and blood, her appearance was a turn-on for audiences spaced out on LSD. "She was the archetypal bitch-goddess of San Francisco mythology," explained one, "Boccaccio's Venus who rose out of the free love ethnic in Haight-Ashbury. She used to remind me of Ava Gardner in the reruns on television of *One Touch of Venus;* the untouchable acid queen, sort of a mirage of femininity."

Ironically, while Grace was coming forward as a public sex symbol, her own husband was becoming indifferent to her. It was a long time in the making, a dwindling of attraction into humdrum habit. Though they were now spending all their time together with everything in common, they had sadly slipped into a domestic cliché of taking each other for granted. By the winter of 1966, their sex life together had diminished to late-night chatter with brief intermissions perhaps once or twice a week. "Every time I'd get turned on," said Jerry, "she'd spend nearly an hour in the bathroom washing her face with Nivea." When she finally came out, his passion had cooled or he lay fast asleep. It went on this way for nearly a year, with a short resurgence of interest when dropping acid added a new dimension to their conversations, but, as she noted at the time, "Jerry is now becoming a better friend than husband."

This change in their relationship was a subtle evolution and Grace had not yet come to terms with it when her unsatisfied needs led her to seek compensation from others. As one of the few and foxiest women on the hip rock scene, she certainly had her pick of the litter, but she curiously settled on a rock musician who, married and a father-to-be, was one of the few who were relatively unavailable.

On a Tuesday evening in January, when the falling temperature was actually frosting the window in their bedroom, Jerry lay on his pillow with his eyes wide open wondering where in the world his wife was. The next morning, with her new inamorato in hand, she walked into their bedroom and announced to her startled husband that they had just spent the night together. Jerry lay there propped up against the pillows trying to keep his cool in front of his wife's lover: a scene out of a marriage which might have been set up by Ingmar Bergman. When Jerry and Grace were alone again, Jerry was livid. "What am I, your father confessor?" he raged. "If you hadn't told me I never would have known about it."

Grace remained silent and thoughtful. "Then it's all right with you," she concluded, "as long as I stay dishonest and sneaky—and don't tell you about it?"

Underlying her sudden and sputtering attractions for other men was the slow realization of the total rejection by her husband. Jerry listened to her standard tune but did not provide a fitting cadenza for it. Grace consequently suffered in silence without full recognition of how his turnoff was diminishing her self-confidence. "In many ways I can't blame Jerry; after all, I was the one who had first proposed years ago. I guess I was all right for a couple of years when he was building up his confidence, but now that he was a man in his own right, I couldn't blame him for wanting to check out the competition. Who wants to get stuck for a lifetime with a sarcastic energy machine who has three-foot knees and a half-inch bosom?"

The days drifted into low-budget and high-energy living with an endless string of gigs at the Matrix, the Fillmore and the Avalon Ballroom, the tacky little nightclub in North Beach where they were, at one point, playing six or seven nights for around $175 a week.

Though admittedly second-rate instrumentalists still, with loose-knit if not sloppy harmonies, the band was becoming recognized for its top-rate original repertoire, although, parenthetically, it was often hard to appreciate the high quality of the songs by the way they were played. Though the themes were basically the same as in the songs of every other band, the Great Society brought a new depth of lyrical experimentation to the scene. Several months before the release of the Beatles' "Rubber Soul," which channeled Eastern rhythms through the mainstream of rock, Darby and Peter were interlacing their own arrangements with the ragas they were learning in their classes in Indian music. Though this Eastern influence was infiltrating the international rock scene, the Great Society was heavier into it than the other San Francisco bands. For Darby and Peter it was not just a trend, but a musical expression of their interior perspective and mystic spirits, and through listening to them Grace integrated the winding inundations of their sitars into the force of her naturally earthy singing style. Additionally, Grace was developing her own unique talents as a stream-of-consciousness lyricist, the Virginia Woolf of acid culture. Besides "White Rabbit" and "Father Bruce" she unraveled her thinking about sex in an unusual song for the day entitled "Often As I May" which reinterpreted her recent fling into the mainstream of rock in what was possibly the first ode to free love in the annals of pop music.

Songwriting was something Grace knew she could do well, but her cockiness unfortunately did not extend to her appraisal of her voice; in fact, she was her own worst critic when it came to singing because, despite the raves of local reviewers and the number of recording executives offering contracts ("for around five dollars"), her peers in the dressing rooms kept telling her that "if I sang any louder I could have earned some extra bread as a foghorn or hog caller."

Though Grace did not know all of the local musicians well, she had at least a passing acquaintance with most of them because "I'd see them backstage and at parties all the time." She and Janis Joplin would exchange a couple of quick sentences when they played the same auditorium. Occasionally she would have a few words with Phil Lesh of the Grateful Dead ("Pigpen, on the other hand, scared me"), or with Jerry Garcia and other musicians on the same bill, "but long, detailed conversations were impossible in the midst of the imposing volume of the music."

Airplane appealed to her because "the guys were straight-looking and had a sense of humor that I was able to connect with. They were droll and sarcastic and well educated. Jorma and Paul were very bright and well read and Jack was a totally unique personality." What knocked out Grace about their music was first and foremost the bass playing of Jack. "I didn't like rock and roll bass at the time because it was too predictable." When Jack played, however, he'd hold one note all the way over to the next note "so I didn't feel as if I were being dropped off a cliff. His notes were played like a hammock drawn together between two trees. I felt I was being transported by a jet engine when I listened to him play—not being bumped by a revolving door."

Backstage nearly a hundred musicians would hover around the dressing rooms like errant knights of the Round Table, indulging in a smorgasbord of marijuana, caps of acid, liquid psychedelics and bottles of wine and Southern Comfort. "It wasn't served on silver trays like the Palo Alto cocktail parties," cracked Grace. "It was no big deal and real natural: a feast of psychedelic delicacies which passed from one hip pocket to another while people were circulating freely."

Everybody else was letting it all hang out but Grace's own inhibitions never quite became unscrewed. Off in a corner, she observed the random first movements of free love. It was a dance of spaced-out bodies: a wild choreography where everybody changed partners through chance encounters. Unfortunately, Grace could never quite pull off this lightweight circulating "unless I drank enough alcohol to blot out my feelings. I can't screw a guy just because I admire the way his ponytail is hung. I guess I was a *lot* more conservative than the other chicks in this respect. I wanted to find out if there was anyone *inside* the body first."

In this climate of discontent with her own marriage, she was trying to let things happen spontaneously. All around her at these get-togethers "we were trying to live according to a different code. We weren't specifically rebelling against our parents. We just wanted to develop values of our own." Unfortunately, her intense personality, combined with her hesitancy, was at odds with this scenario. Though she knew what she was supposed to do, "when I'd walk into the dressing room and see hundreds of people milling around I'd get nervous because I always wanted *everybody* to like me. In this size crowd, I sort of figured that I was never going to connect so I just withdrew before anybody realized that I wasn't going to complete the performance."

In these halcyon days of sunshine (natural and chemical), when the love bugs lighted up the finest marijuana around the dressing rooms, she had tried her hand at circulating, "but twenty people all talking at once was too distracting, so I just began to disconnect." Eventually the other people began to notice Grace Slick sitting alone in the corner humming; in fact, she was growing into an enigma on the rock scene, her withdrawal interpreted as her own style of haughtiness.

Grace did, however, derive enormous satisfaction from performing on stage, though not for the typical reasons of earning money or attaining fame. "I don't think of myself as a singer. When I get out on stage I become a musical instrument that just happens to have words coming out of it. If you want to translate lyrics into an integral component of a song, you have to play the lyrics like an instrument. Sometimes you perform them for the meaning of the words, and other times you have to project them as sounds in reaction to the sounds of the other musicians, or match an intonation to the feeling of the lyric."

She wrote her songs with an interesting and unexpected choice of vocabulary. One of her most haunting ballads, entitled "Didn't Think So," evokes the imagery of Edgar Allan Poe in a song about her own experience with a lover. "I didn't write it with any one specific relationship in mind, but rather I combined my experiences with three different men."

She evidenced two unparalleled qualities in the rock music of her day. In songs like "White Rabbit" and "Father Bruce" she impregnated the lyrics with a dramatic quality which combined both strength and seductiveness. According to Herb Caen of the San Francisco *Chronicle:* "When she performed her lyrics like an intricate soliloquy, you had to put down your drink and sit up and listen. She managed to impress you with the importance of what she was saying solely by the magnetism of her presence." In other compositions like "Somebody to Love," "Born to Be Burned" and "Sally Goes Round the Roses" she transmuted the lyrics into the rhythms so that the words performed as the notes of instruments.

This ability to develop a rapport with the instruments impressed even the most sophisticated critics like Ralph Gleason, who marveled at the way she could turn herself into a vocal instrument and soar with the rhythmic flow of her songs. By the summer of 1966, when Janis Joplin had claimed the status of local Earth Mother, Grace was becoming recognized as local Muse, the Euterpe of San Francisco rock who embodied the glacial character of the music in her vocal metamorphoses through the songs. "Nobody ever compared Joplin and me back then," she clarified. "We were as different as asparagus and pomegranates."

In many ways, Grace on stage was the Apollo of her day; the comparison was originally made by Ralph Gleason, who could never quite believe her versatility. "If you can play one instrument," she once told him, "you can play any of them. You just have to pick it up, relax and let it go." Despite her ubiquity on stage, where she hopped from recorder to bass to organ to guitar in performing the different songs, "I never had a secure foundation as a musician. I was only able to perform improvisations since I had never taken any lessons."

Herb Caen was struck (if not knocked out) by her beauty the first time he saw the Great Society in performance. "It was like watching Elizabeth Taylor playing bass," he recalled. "What she brought to this new stage of rock was a touch of class."

Predictably, by the summer she already had a cult following, though, according to Ben Fong-Torres, "a lot of us never really were too impressed by her since we didn't go to the clubs to listen to the music. The bands were just an excuse for scoring acid."

Her reputation grew throughout 1966 until she began being recognized on the streets by acidheads who let it all hang out at the dances, "but when they ran into me in the parking lot or supermarket, they were awfully disappointed if I didn't act as if I had just climbed out of a tree. I had the feeling that they wanted me to do something crazy and if I didn't, no matter how pleasant I was to them, they walked away disappointed."

Days spent relaxing among the hippies in Golden Gate Park were a distraction from the ongoing beat of rehearsals and a steady stream of gigs from their opening at Mother's through the week-long stints at the Matrix and the weekend Trips Festivals at the Longshoreman's Hall, culminating under the high ceilings of the Fillmore, the Liberty Hall of the counterculture. "At the time it was just fun and music. If I had known Arnold Toynbee and Will Durant were going to interpret this period as an American Renaissance, I would have kept a real diary." Back then, none of us thought about a court recorder for what was happening. There was no countercultural didactic. We just did it. Nobody stopped to figure out what was going on: we just drifted with the flow. We didn't want to rewrite history. None of us ever thought that way; but now that I think of it we probably wouldn't have minded redirecting it."

The Great Society in the summer of 1966 was playing mostly at the Avalon Ballroom and the Fillmore, where Jerry would negotiate with Bill Graham, "who I thought was a pretty reasonable guy," Jerry said. "He was paying $2,500 for three bands on the bill. When I asked him for more money for us, he just said he was giving us all he could. So there was no sense arguing because I didn't want the man to go bankrupt; besides, the money was never very important to our band. We were dead broke but pretty happy at that time because guys from Los Angeles were starting to come backstage and tell us we were going to make it."

Their relationship with their manager Donahue gradually loosened because "he was pretty heavy into the drug scene and not taking care of business. When we told him we wanted to find another manager, he got into a legal fiasco with us claiming all our material was his; but things cooled down pretty fast because the music business was still a very loose and friendly scene."

Around this time musician and founding father Jack Nitzsche expressed interest in the band "and the fact that he wanted to get involved with us nearly blew us away," said Jerry. Nitzsche was one of the behind-the-scenes stars of the control room in the recording studios of Los Angeles. He had been working as the arranger for Phil Spector and even played occasional backup on the albums of the Rolling Stones; in fact, back in 1963, he had arranged twenty-six different records which made the pop charts. Jerry and Darby went out of their minds but Grace was unimpressed. "How do you know if he's right for us?"

As it turned out, Nitzsche turned them off because his first prerequisite was a change of name. "We weren't opposed to canning the Great Society," Jerry said, "but we couldn't stand the name he was planning for our baptism in the national record scene. It was something like the Candy Machine or the Candy Factory, which made all of us sick."

Nitzsche was loose about the recording deal because "he wasn't too concerned about what we would do on an album. He just wanted to release 'Somebody to Love' as a single. We figured the guy would make us into a national band, but who wanted to live out life as the Monkees? So we just bided our time until another hotshot came along."

The hotshot turned out to be Howard Wolfe, who signed them to an exclusive contract. "His prime qualification for the band was his temperament," Jerry recalls. "He didn't scream a lot and he was low-pressure. We figured we could live with him—and the contract with Columbia Records for an advance of $50,000." (RCA had paid the Airplane $40,000 a few months earlier.)

As the activity began to brew around the band, it became apparent that the musicians needed to intensify their rehearsing to get a tighter sound. Darby suggested that the musicians live together in a commune, so they all moved into a rambling old house in Mill Valley and began the undisciplined "family style" setup, with Grace claiming the master bedroom with attaching "private" bathroom for Jerry and herself. In these close quarters, the songs improved but the personnel fell apart. There were fights about the groceries, chores and even the cleaning. "Grace went crazy about the loss of privacy," recalls Jerry. "She felt as if she had nowhere to go and hide."

The internal friction in the house carried over into their discussions about music. Darby and Peter were still studying Indian ragas and getting heavily into Eastern strains; in fact, they were even talking about taking a sabbatical from the stage and going to India to learn from the masters. Though Grace enjoyed the Eastern influence, "we were a Western band, and trying to imitate a culture we had never seen was not one of my favorite ideas. They were a little too enthusiastic about Indian music for me," she said. At the heart of the dissension, though, was the growing recognition that "none of us were anywhere near being professional musicians."

"After we played a gig at the Avalon Ballroom with the Blues Project, she went crazy," said Jerry. "She wanted to sing with a tighter band and better musicians. She wanted to work with other vocalists to weave intricate harmonies into the fabric of the songs." She also wanted out of the communal house.

Her frustrations increased as she began to compare the Great Society with the other bands around. "After I heard the Blues Project, I knew what I wanted to do," she explained, "but it wouldn't be possible to cram five years of musical knowledge into two months in order to open up our band with intricate harmonies and improvisations." The only band on the scene professional enough was Jefferson Airplane; by the fall of 1966, they had polished up their three-part harmonies, and the originality of Jorma Kaukonen's guitar playing had even struck a chord with Jerry Garcia, who, it was rumored, followed him around with a tape recorder. The idea of singing through the rhythms of Jorma's guitar excited and intrigued Grace, "and I began thinking about what it would be like to sing with those musicians."

Ironically, her rapport with them was minimal, casual and polite. "They were aloof like me," she explained, "so while I didn't talk much to them, I could understand where they were coming from."

By September, the Great Society had fired David Minor, Peter and Darby were talking more and more about studying music in India and Jerry was itching to get back to his camera. In a typical but sad paradox common on the music scene, as the band moved closer to the forefront, its members were fragmenting.

And then Jack Casady, speaking for the Airplane, came backstage one night and asked Grace if she might be interested in joining up with *them*. All of a sudden it was a whole new show.

6

Darby and Peter would rather play ragas than rock songs, and Jerry would rather make movies than music. Grace was the only one who still wanted to perform rock and roll, and since the Airplane had invited her aboard, there was no reason not to go. Jerry agreed, and thus was disbanded, the Great Society.

Jerry had little to say about the new situation, and Grace took his silence as a sign of relieved acquiescence. Darby was not quite so understanding, and felt that, in effect, Grace was deserting them. It was one thing for him to want to expand his range of musical knowledge by going off to India, but the idea of Grace actually defecting from his band was a high act of treason.

Logistics took the heat off the moment as they all moved out of the commune, which they quickly unrented, and went their separate ways. Grace and Jerry found a modest unfurnished apartment on DeHaro Street back in the city. In Mill Valley, without benefit of epitaph or tombstone, the Great Society was buried quietly; an untimely death in October 1966, canceling their record contract with Columbia. Had the band lived it might have been a prime factor in the growth of San Francisco rock; the unrecorded mass of materials left behind and never revived equaled, if not surpassed, the songs of other longer-lasting and better-known bands. The only lasting memorabilia of their performances turned out to be tapes of their early gigs at Mother's which were sold to Columbia Records by the club's owner Peter Abrahm. The quality of the sound is poor due to the original mechanism for taping; the composite is rough-edged and the interpretation still in need of refinement; but despite the drawbacks the album, first issued as a single record and then as a set, continues to appeal to a few appreciators of the originality of the cuts. It remains the only specter of what might have been.

Darby left for India and Jerry reestablished connections in advertising. Over the next few months he began shooting commercials for Kellogg, Chrysler and Aqua Velva, ironically winning a Clio award for his cinematography on a commercial for the recruitment of San Francisco police in 1971, and eventually getting elected to the Cowboy Hall of Fame for his historical series on California. Meanwhile Grace headed in a different direction. As Jerry got out his camera, she took off for Fell Street to meet the Airplane in an apartment where Marty Balin and Jack Casady were sharing a "longitudinal" arrangement with the territorial imperative in sections. Grace was naturally very impressed by this individual kind of rooming situation where everybody had his own space. "In the front area was Marty's room with more art than furniture; in fact, it had enough little sculptures in every corner to fill a gallery." In contrast, Jack's space in the middle of the flat was clean and neat and, she noted attentively, came with a very pretty but temporary roommate, a young woman named Ginger who had previously lived (on different occasions) with Paul Kantner and Ken Kesey.

The reasons behind Signe Toly Anderson's leaving the group had been complicated, an inevitable conclusion to a growing conflict. Signe had just given birth to a daughter. Her husband, who functioned as the Airplane's lighting man, had been threatening to withdraw his wife from the group if they didn't make special concessions to her. They gave in on a couple of his demands but got tired of that after a while, and eventually agreed that while they liked Signe and her talents, they just couldn't put up with her husband. "I figured what they were doing with her had nothing to do with me," said Grace. "I just assumed she wanted to leave the band because she had just started a family."

It was Paul, who played rhythm guitar and talent scout for the band, who had brought up Grace's name as a possible replacement. "I've always liked strong women who could sing," he admitted, "so I used to go around to the different clubs to check out the competition as a pastime." Oddly enough, he was too shy to talk to her himself, and like a scene out of *Cyrano de Bergerac,* he asked the more outgoing Jack Casady to speak to her directly. "Jack became my first friend in the group," Grace said. "I felt very comfortable when he was around." It was Jack who performed the introductions to the other musicians, which was nothing very formal "since I had met them all backstage several times and used to spot Paul hanging out when the Great Society played. I had even rapped with them at parties, but we weren't very tight with each other."

The preliminaries dealt with, Grace was now a member of the Jefferson Airplane. Bill Graham, who was by then managing Airplane (after a litigious parting with their first manager, Matthew Katz), had to negotiate with Bill Thompson for the legal rights to Grace, who was then technically the artistic property of Howard Wolfe, who still had the Great Society under contract. Graham bought Grace for $750 but Wolfe wisely retained the rights to the songs of the Great Society which the Airplane planned to recycle into their own repertoire.

When Grace returned home, one of Jerry's first concerns was how much money she would be getting as a member of the group. Grace honestly didn't know and frankly didn't care. She'd find out soon enough when she received her first check, she figured; besides, how could they rip her off if money didn't matter to her? The Great Society had been a band born out of amateur enthusiasm, while the Airplane was piloted by experienced musicians who had spent their pre-flight time tuning up in the folk, jazz and even the burlesque clubs. Paul Kantner had started playing guitar on the folk circuit back in the University of Santa Clara and had once gotten together a trio with David Freiberg, who later started Quicksilver Messenger Service, and David Crosby, who hooked up with the Byrds. Paul was playing in San Francisco as a solo at the Drinking Gourd when Marty Balin, who had quit the folk group the Town Criers, struck up a conversation with him and asked if he were interested in starting a folk rock band. Since Kantner's friends Jim (Roger) McGuinn and David Crosby had just hit pay dirt with the Byrds, "I had some attraction to the idea," he said. Marty invited him to drop by his apartment the next afternoon for a jam session and Kantner replied with a characteristic "Maybe."

When he got there, several musicians, including a tone-deaf classical guitarist whom nobody had seen before or has heard from since, were really into it. Kantner joined in and tried different arrangements of songs like "Tobacco Road" and "Wild Child." Afterward he stuck around "because Marty and I got along fine in that situation and I wanted to see how things would work out." A few weeks earlier, Balin had found some medical doctors willing to invest in a new rock club which they wanted to call the Matrix. "I had a vision of amplified guitars with drums for years," Balin admitted. "It was very unusual for the times since drums were out of it in 1965. I wanted to open a club with my own band in residence but I never had the bread. Then one night these girls who used to come by and hear me sing at the Drinking Gourd brought along these guys who, in conversation, told me they had nine thousand dollars for the project."

As Marty supervised the reconstruction of the club on Fillmore Street, Kantner began to recruit musicians for the band. His first phone call was to Jorma Kaukonen, whom he had met on the beach surfing in Santa Cruz through mutual friends at the University of Santa Clara, where Jorma had graduated with a sociology degree. In the following years, Jorma had made a minor reputation as a blues guitarist in the Bay area: a cult figure with a small but devoted following who played his first gig at the Folk Theatre in San Jose with Steve Talbot, Billy Roberts and Janis Joplin. He and Joplin became something of a duo act around the club circuit—"in fact, she was responsible for my first solo gig," he recalled, "when she failed to show up for our act at the Tangent in Palo Alto." The two kept on performing together for several months. "It was because of her that I switched from acoustic to electric guitar," he said. "She was so loud that I couldn't compete with her without it."

Curiously, Kantner and Kaukonen had never played together in their early days "because we were into different kinds of music. He was into heavy blues and I was more the Pete Seeger

type," said Kantner, "and that put us into different categories.
When Marty told me to find someone, though, I immediately
thought of Jorma because he was such a good musician. I figured
what difference does it make if we don't play the same kind of
music. It will probably only last one night anyway."

At the Drinking Gourd Kantner and Balin had long admired
the rich resonance of Signe Toly, a dark-haired and often pig-
tailed naturalist whose renditions of folk songs were in the tradition of the strong-voiced Mary Travis rather than the airier Judy
Collins or Joan Baez. Signe had a deep and stirring vibrato
which, Kantner felt, could add vocal texture—not to mention visual adornment—to the band. Kantner wanted to have a woman
on stage with the group because "I like the combination of male
and female. Girl singers are my favorite kind of women since
most of them are strong. They have to be to get away with it."
Signe took their invitation to join the resident band of a nonexistent club as a lark and agreed on the spot to sing harmonies
with Marty and Paul.

By the time Grace got into the act, the band had been born
and re-formed. Bassist Bob Harvey had been replaced by Jack
Casady, whom Jorma had recruited from Washington, D.C. The
two of them had played in high school at the local bars there
and stayed in touch when Jorma came west and Jack got into
teaching guitar. Skip Spence gave notice after nine months of
playing drums for the band. Trained as a guitarman, he wanted
to perform on his original instrument and eventually left Airplane to start up the band Moby Grape. As a replacement, the
band imported Spencer Dryden from Los Angeles, who came
highly recommended by Earl Palmer, a well-known studio musician. Spencer had been playing at the strip club called the Trip
and recently in the rock band called Ashes when he came up to
San Francisco and got talked into staying over a couple of drinks
at Enrico's.

In barely a year on the scene, this offbeat and eclectic mixture
of musicians had soared far ahead of the other bands—despite
their funky name which came from Steve Talbot, a blues singer
in Berkeley, who was thinking of "unusual" names for musicians

in a blues band and created the nomenclature Blind Thomas Jefferson Airplane. Jorma heard it and repeated it to the band in jest, "and we used it," Marty recalled, "even though we all thought it was weird, nobody came up with anything better."

Their name was not the only thing different about them and, incidentally, it stood them in good stead because it brought them to immediate attention as the "weirdest-sounding band at any gig." Their flight log that first year, between 1965 and 1966, was a schedule of unrouted stops at the major festivals throughout the country. What was interesting about their course was their tendency to weave in and out of different genres of music. Previously folk, rock, jazz and classical music played out their lives in concerts in different camps with separate audiences; but Airplane single-handedly began to break down those barriers in this country as leading pioneers of eclectic electric pop music.

On July 3 the Airplane became the first rock band to participate in a seminar and perform in concert at the Berkeley Folk Festival (with Pete Seeger in residence). Of their performance wrote Bill Haigwood of the Berkeley *Gazette:* "The three vocalists Paul Kantner, pretty Signe Anderson and Marty Balin, after fighting chronic microphone trouble, shouted, wailed and bellowed a sensational series of sounds which in rock and roll add up only to 'the sound.'"

Through Ralph Gleason they received an unprecedented invitation that September to perform, amid jazzmen like Duke Ellington and Count Basie, at the Monterey Jazz Festival. More than important exposure to the highbrow critics, their appearance signaled a revolution in the culture which several of the most eminent critics and fans resisted. "Does rock and roll have a valid place in a jazz festival?" asked Leonard Feather, who made their performance into a major issue through the pages of the Los Angeles *Times.* "The answer was provided at the Monterey Jazz Festival here Saturday afternoon. It is a resounding, roaring, amplified, hyperthyroid 'no.'" He went on in his article to attack the band "with its raunchy voices and reverberating guitars." He wrote: "Jefferson Airplane . . . never got off the ground. Perhaps there were too many strings attached. Its

sledge-hammer rhythm, monotonous melodious concepts and almost nonexistent harmony have all the delicacy and finesse of a
mule team knocking down a picket fence."

The band was simply amused by the review; for all the controversy engendered through their performance, the musicians were
swiftly coming to symbolize the revolution of the modern culture. Their rising status was evidenced in the increasing number
of phone calls Bill Thompson (who was acting road manager by
then) was getting from important people in the business. One
morning while he was still in his bathrobe, he picked up the
phone to hear the "unmistakable voice of Ed Sullivan." Personally and without benefit of his secretary, Sullivan extended an
invitation to appear on his television show, "but when I hung up
I realized Ed never gave me a date," Thompson said, "and he
didn't ever call back again." Shortly after he hung up, within
days, he received a second call, "just as I was getting out of the
shower," from Colonel Parker, who wanted to know if the band
would be interested in becoming the opening act for Elvis.
Parker did follow up with a letter "but we never heard from
him again either. I was beginning to wonder if I didn't have bad
telephone breath!"

The third telephone call blew the minds of the musicians, for
finally it was a *firm* offer, to appear as the opening act for the
Rolling Stones at the Cow Palace—the major show of the year in
that area. As it turned out, the Rolling Stones said no when they
heard about the Airplane, since the Stones traveled with their
own opening band. As a result, Airplane got ousted from this sa-
cred position and moved down to the second of the four bands
on the bill.

Despite their recognition on the national scene, like every family of man Airplane was having domestic problems behind the
scenes. On its first tour in Chicago things finally came to a head
as they got ready to play the backstreet club Mother Blues. "We
were staying at the Hotel Cass—boy, what a dump," recalled
Thompson, who was then on the road for the first time. "There
were two in a room and twenty-five cockroaches to every bed.
We were paying twenty bucks a pair and even at that rate it was
overpriced."

Since money was tight—"we each had about ten dollars in our pockets and the thousand-dollar check from the club eventually bounced—each of the musicians was traveling solo except for Signe who brought along her three-month-old daughter and her husband with the band paying for them. Ten minutes after we arrived," recalled Thompson, "when we were trying to get the equipment together, Signe realized the suitcase for the baby was missing. So with the band about to make its national debut, I had to run around looking for diapers."

After the show the guys hung out at Big John's, a blues club, until the wee hours of the morning, when they rolled into their rooms. "As I closed my eyes at around 3 A.M., the telephone rang," said Thompson. On the other end of the wire was Signe, who had been trying to reach Bill for hours to tell him she was quitting. "She kept repeating that she couldn't have a family and keep on touring. She was hysterical and I spent an hour and a half trying to calm her down."

Thompson was up the rest of the night trying to figure out what to do. He roused his roommate Marty and together they phoned Bill Graham and RCA in the morning. "To get her to stay we offered her special privileges and higher pay than the rest of us and she finally agreed to accept on those conditions. The next night she showed up at the club with the baby on her lap." Thompson ended up baby-sitting during the gig.

When he got back to San Francisco, Thompson phoned up Ralph Gleason to ask about how he should deal with Signe. Gleason listened patiently and then summarized the situation in a single sentence: "Every band with a female singer has had problems."

Enter Grace blithely innocent and oblivious to the daily soap opera. Though she accepted their offer at the beginning of October, none of the musicians had yet broken the news to Signe. Out of guilt they decided to award her six thousand dollars' severance pay over a period of a year and then elected Thompson, who was absent during the balloting, to tell her.

On the afternoon after they played a benefit for the Haight-Ashbury Free Clinic at the Fillmore, Thompson drove over to

Eighth Avenue, where Signe was playing with her baby in her house. "I felt like the Iceman Cometh," said Thompson, "and I tried to be real gentle with her. I just told her that nobody in the band wanted to perform with both her and her husband and the baby any more."

She digested the news slowly and stoically at first, "but then when I mentioned Grace Slick was taking her place, she kept repeating that we just wanted to get rid of her because we preferred Grace to her. Finally I couldn't stand it any more so I told her the truth. It wasn't Grace we preferred, we just couldn't stand her husband."

By the time Thompson walked out the door, she was calmer since he had promised her the six thousand dollars. He drove, low on gas and conscience-stricken, back to his apartment, where, coincidentally, the entire band was rehearsing, smoking and hanging out waiting to hear "how she took it." Thompson played his role of herald like a character out of Shakespeare. He milked every line in his stellar performance for the band; in fact, he relived the sequence of events with such tedious detail that Spencer went out for a drink. When he came back, Bill was still talking "and I swear I didn't miss any of it." Still feeling guilty, the musicians agreed to send her a "big" bouquet of flowers on stage at the Fillmore on Saturday.

In the background, meanwhile, Grace was off practicing . . . alone. For weeks she had been listening to the band's initial album entitled *Jefferson Airplane Takes Off*, which, incidentally, was the first major recording of any San Francisco band. Though destined to become a collector's item, it came in for a quick landing at the time of its release early in September when it reportedly sold only twenty thousand copies (mostly in the Bay area— and mainly to local folkies who felt a special tie to the band).

In her living room during the afternoons, Grace was wearing out her turntable by playing the songs over and over again and trying to figure out Signe's part in them. "She only had one rich solo in the song 'Chauffeur Blues' and the band cut that from the repertoire. So I was essentially coming on as a background vocalist for Marty doing harmonies with Paul—and adding some songs from the Great Society like 'White Rabbit' and 'Somebody to Love' as backups."

The days drifted into anxiety. "It was no easy challenge to learn how to sing with a band when you have never rehearsed with them," she said. Signe was still performing and participating in rehearsals, and the musicians, trying to keep things cool, told Grace to stay away. Finally one afternoon Signe went to the doctor with her baby and Grace went to her first rehearsal with the Airplane. "Things were so loose in Jack's apartment that day that I couldn't believe anything ever got accomplished in this group. Marty would be talking about this beautiful phrase in a poem he had just read and asking if Paul thought he could write rhythms around it. Meanwhile Paul was talking to Jorma about a song he had sung three weeks ago. 'I think you should add a twelve string in the second part,' he'd say. Jorma nodded but later admitted he didn't remember a note of it.

"The conversations were running on five separate tracks with no coherent theme binding them together. You could tune into several different conversations at once and really enjoy them but it didn't get the band anywhere; however, one positive thing I can say about the chaos was that everybody was open to every suggestion. When I walked out of that two-hour session, I had still not sung a single song from start to finish."

At the instruction of Jack, she started hanging out backstage with the band at every gig to learn the repertoire by watching it being performed, "sort of like a rookie on the bench," she said, "warming up for the big play."

On October 14 when she walked backstage into the Fillmore to hang out Paul rushed over to her. Signe hadn't shown up. "Do you think you can do it?" he asked. Ten minutes later Spencer came over and hugged her, then Thompson eased up and told her he thought she was going to be marvelous.

"I really wasn't ready but I guess I figured it was only rock and roll and why not." Without choosing special clothes or adding make-up, she stepped out on stage to perform with them, "and the first thing that struck me was how loud they were. Ten times louder than the Great Society. I couldn't hear myself singing. I had no idea what notes I was hitting; I just hoped that if they were wrong at least they wouldn't be too loud. It was grotesque if you looked at it from the point of view of singing in tune. But it was, as I said, only rock and roll, and the audience seemed to enjoy the novelty of a new singer. They were very polite, or else they were very tone-deaf."

7

The debut at the Fillmore Auditorium was inauspicious, but Grace wasn't particularly undone by it because, apparently, "nobody heard how bad I was." The other musicians were self-absorbed and the audience was tripping; only Bill Thompson rushed over to "tell me I was 'marvelous,' and that they had stepped up rehearsals to four hours a day . . ."

The extra work was preparation for the group's next recording session in Los Angeles which was barely two weeks away. *Jefferson Airplane Takes Off* had been released in August without making a dent in the national market. Still, the RCA executives in the boardrooms in New York made the decision to continue their investment. It was written in the winds of the industry (and in the July 1, 1966, *Time* magazine) that the next trend would blow off the San Francisco Bay.

Compared to the other musicians around, Airplane were masters of the as yet unformulated San Francisco genre. In a scene where every concert was a happening because neither audiences nor club owners ever knew if the musicians would even show up, Airplane was *together*. It was consequently everybody's bet that they would eventually become the official heralds of the San Francisco Sound, whatever it was.

In the fall of 1966 much new music was being played, defining the trends to come: the Byrds were beginning to breed their folk rock with elements of science fiction and a general outer space approach to rock in general, the Lovin' Spoonful was hitting with their countrified harmonies, Simon and Garfunkel were discovering their own poetry in songwriting, the Blues Project were living jazz rock at the Village Gate in Manhattan, combining the talents of Al Kooper and Mike Bloomfield, Dylan had solidified his rock work with *Blonde on Blonde,* and, perhaps most importantly (and commercially), the Beatles had released *Revolver* (coincidentally the same week as *Jefferson Airplane Takes Off*), their most serious album to date, demonstrating their mastery of studio techniques and their willingness to experiment. Against this background of classic rock recordings, northern California still had a long way to go to make its own contributions. Local groups like Mystery Train and others were further out than the Beatles would ever be, but their lack of stage charisma and plain bad luck kept them from ever getting a chance to record their music. Nevertheless, they were exploring some of the most avant-garde areas of rock and roll. They just never lasted long enough to make an impression.

Despite the high-flown praise of *Crawdaddy,* which claimed that *Jefferson Airplane Takes Off* was "perhaps the best rock album ever produced," the album (by virtue of hindsight) was little more than a sampling of the group's future abilities. The musical craftsmanship was there but formulaic. The lyrics, while tapping the fount of popular appeal, never quite touched the experience of the individual musicians. The album unraveled like a superficial collection of popular poems: a lush fabric of beautiful textures still untailored and too unsophisticated to form an intricate tapestry. Still, there are a few pregnant moments: notably, the soft-spoken yearning of Marty Balin on "Come Up the Years," not yet matured into his later tender romanticism; the footloose improvisations of Signe Toly Anderson on "Chauffeur Blues"; and Jorma Kaukonen's swaggering guitar on "Let Me In" and "Tobacco Road." Unfortunately, the rest of the songs were simply contrived and/or derivative.

By the time they began writing songs for their second album, Spencer Dryden had brought to the group a new jazz consciousness and Grace her talent for writing lyrics. As a result, the other musicians slowly started to deepen their own insights through *their* lyrics. "We were writing songs which revealed what we were feeling and thinking," Grace recalls of that period, "not what the executives thought would sell."

Amid all this creative furor, the girl friends of the musicians used to hang around the Fillmore, where the group was rehearsing, in effect a nice expanded family group. Ginger especially noticed Grace's growing interest in Jack Casady. Things being what they were, they made a sort of deal. According to Grace: "She told me she would get him in San Francisco, and I could get him down the road in L.A."

Bill Thompson arrived early for the flight to L.A. for the recording sessions since he was in charge of ticketing. As he turned around from the counter, there was Grace. It was her habit always to arrive early for any appointment; she would usually get there twenty minutes to a half hour before the other guys. So Thompson was not surprised to see her. "It was what she was wearing that blew my mind." She had dressed to go Hollywood, which signaled to her long-haired wig, spike heels, nylons, the whole Beverly Hills ensemble. "I tried to reason with her," said Thompson, "and tell her that girls in rock and roll bands do not dress that way." But Grace made it clear that her appearance was not negotiable.

The other musicians slowly began to appear, one by one, in their own different styles. Spencer Dryden showed up at the ticket counter slightly hung over in his black cowboy suit. Paul Kantner, looking unstarched but preppie, carried his craftsy briefcase filled with Oreos. Marty Balin strolled in with a volume of French poetry tucked under his elbow.

Ten minutes before the flight, Jack Casady and Jorma Kaukonen still had not appeared. By this time Thompson was a wreck. Nervously he made the decision to board the plane. He turned to pick up Grace's bags and felt her sandal crushing his foot. "I carry them," she said, later explaining: "I figured if I let any of them help me, they would expect me to cook a little something for them on the side . . ." Casady and Kaukonen arrived at the last minute, blithely ignorant of having caused any hassles.

The band members scattered upon landing in Los Angeles to carry out their respective tasks. There were no fan clubs clamoring for their attention at the airport, no chauffeured limousines waiting to whisk them off to hotel suites. Instead Thompson arranged for two budget rent-a-cars. Marty loaded equipment. Grace carried guitars. Jack and Spencer ran around gathering baggage. Paul and Jorma drove.

Around the long, winding stretches of Los Angeles, they sped past the lavish palm trees of the Beverly Hills Hotel and the first-class luxury high-rises of the Sunset Strip down to the Tropicana, which, at twelve dollars a night, was the Grand Hotel of Santa Monica Boulevard and the overnight haunt of would-be rock stars. "Jim Morrison was there when we were. At one point he was naked, crawling around the halls, barking like a dog—in other words, being very Jim Morrison." Each member of the band got his own poolside room equipped with a kitchenette. An hour after check-in, while the guys were busy phoning their ladies for the evening, Grace was filling her cart in Ralph's Supermarket. She loaded up on orange juice, eggs, bacon, English muffins, tea and raspberry junket, which she ate every chance she could. After she put away her groceries she grabbed a bottle of wine and went to knock on Jack's door to bum a corkscrew . . .

Grace arrived at the studio early the next night, at 7:30 P.M. October 31, to watch the producer and engineer in the control room. She sat off in a corner sewing with one eye cast on the board. "My impression was that the producer and engineer came attached to the knobs."

On the first album the band had recorded for four days in the tiny and less instrumentally sophisticated Studio C. The rescheduling of the Airplane to Studio A was interpreted correctly as a corporate nod of approval and a sign of increasing investment in them. The vote of confidence came, as previously mentioned, as a result of their firm endorsement by *Time*. In an article on the modern lyrics in rock, the writer focused first on analyzing Bob Dylan's "Rainy Day Women ♯12 & ♯35," then hopped to the songs of Jefferson Airplane, whom he casually identified as "San Francisco's most popular rock 'n' roll group."

Naturally this sort of promise in print struck the hearts of the executives, who were then making their first excursion into ex-

Above,
Grace's debut, for an audience
of two—her mother and father.
Photo by Ivan Wing.

Right,
Virginia Barnett,
aspiring actress and singer.
Photo courtesy of Virginia Wing.

Above,
Ivan and Grace.
Photo courtesy of Virginia Wing.

Right,
fantasy time.
Photo by Ivan Wing.

A contemplative pose. *Photo by Ivan Wing.*

Above,
Grace's composite from
her modeling portfolio.
Photo courtesy of Grace Johnson.

Right,
Mr. and Mrs. Jerry Slick.
Photo courtesy of Virginia Wing.

The Great Society. From left: Jerry Slick, David Miner, Grace Slick, Darby Slick, Bard Du Pont. *Photo courtesy of Virginia Wing.*

Photo courtesy of Jefferson Starship.

The original Jefferson Airplane. From left: Jorma Kaukonen, Jerry Peloquin, Signe
Anderson, Bob Harvey, Marty Balin, Paul Kantner. *Photo courtesy of RCA.*

fferson Airplane with Grace Slick, from the *Surrealistic Pillow* era. From left: Paul
antner, Jorma Kaukonen, Marty Balin, Spencer Dryden, Jack Casady, Grace Slick.
oto courtesy of RCA.

Right, a promo shot.
Photo courtesy of RCA.

Below, performing.
Photo courtesy of RCA.

perimental rock. For years the company had been resting on the
laurels planted by the gold albums of Elvis Presley, whose
sales had been underwriting the entire division. Otherwise, the
record company was still pretty straight and middle-of-the-road;
but as DJ Neely Plumb advised his cohorts from his turntable in
San Francisco, pop music was quickly veering left, and through
the Airplane RCA was moving knee-deep into a new musical
stream.

Back in their cushioned offices in New York, where pictures of
Eddie Fisher, Neil Sedaka and Paul Anka still hung high on the
walls, the recording executives did not give much thought to the
social revolution in Haight-Ashbury until they quietly and slowly
realized that the values of the underground were infiltrating the
lyrics on their albums. With ten thousand albums of *Jefferson
Airplane Takes Off* about to roll off the presses, the executives
began to analyze the lyrics of the song "Running 'Round the
World" and found, to their straitlaced amazement, that it was
about an acid trip. An emergency meeting was called where they
boiled down their decision whether or not to censor to this question: "Would General Sarnoff ever notice it?"

With fates hanging in the wind, they finally decided to cut it.
The reason cited was the specific line: "The nights I've spent
with you have been fantastic trips." The censorship was made on
the basis that the company did not want to encourage the taking
of drugs. The A & R men informed the band about the excision
with all the delicacy of henchmen. The Airplane reacted as if
they had been guillotined; but contractually they were impotent
to stop the butchering of their songs. Thus was born a rivalry
which the corporation was to live to regret.

Rick Jarrard was not involved in the censoring; in fact, he was
unaware of the past history when he was assigned as an in-house
producer to tailor the group's next venture. Though he eventually went on to become a top producer in the industry for Harry
Nilsson and later José Feliciano, for whom he produced the legendary *Light My Fire* in 1966, Jarrard was then a fresh-scrubbed
face, out of a singing group in the Middle West, with bright blue
eyes, hefty build and a straight "technical" personality. The band

disparaged him behind his back as an automaton and a company man but in the studio during recording he was unquestionably in command. "None of us knew anything about the technical stuff," Grace explained, "so we just sang and played the instruments and left the turning of the knobs to him."

Jarrard was in charge of the technical aspects, but the Airplane did their own decorating, to soften the cold atmosphere of the recording studio, draping scarves over the equipment and burning sticks of incense planted on the sound baffles. In between cuts, when Jarrard gave them a few minutes to relax, the musicians mostly sat back and lit up. When Jarrard realized they were smoking marijuana, he firmly forbid it. Though it was not written in the fine print of the contract, drugs were not allowed during recording sessions in the studio—yet. This infringement on their personal habits was unacceptable. Not only did they refuse to obey but they decided not to have Jarrard work on any of their future albums. Their anger with the corporation was ironically but nevertheless predictably an enlivenment of their musical sensibility, for their new album would be a declaration of independence from the establishment. What Airplane originated was a romanticism for the electronic age: aural prisms of an afternoon in Haight-Ashbury through a modern poetry of alienation: the T. S. Eliots for the now generation. Through the exotic wailings of Jorma Kaukonen's electronic guitar, they transmuted their thoughts into the first chords of the music later tagged "acid rock" by the straight critics in New York.

Unlike the highly homogenized harmonies of the Beach Boys, for example, Airplane never strived for a synthesis of its divergent sensibilities. Through the arrangements of each song, there remain strains of the individual styles of the musicians. What evolves is an intriguing unity of oppositions which creates unusual breadth and original interplay within each structure. The sophistication of this eclecticism had seldom been heard on the rock scene before. Though the Beatles were moving in this direction with the release of *Revolver,* concentrating on the integrity of each song rather than the formulaic harmonies of the band, *rock* groups rarely worked so creatively. For most, success in the business meant coming up with one "golden" sound and playing it to death. Airplane, conversely, sought a different formula for every song.

The recording sessions began with the laying down of tracks on the light lyrical "My Best Friend," composed by their ex-drummer Skip (Alex) Spence. Spence was going through some hard times and the guys included it to help out a good friend. To overshadow the redundancy of the lyrics, they arranged the song with quick tempo changes building into a short-lived counter-point with the complementary vocal qualities of Grace and Marty. The song was recorded in only four takes, and they turned their attention to the more complicated "She Has Funny Cars," which eventually introduced the album. The vocals are haunted by the resonance of Grace's alto woven around Marty's lead. Marty wrote the song, a minor epic on modern love, in three separate movements. It took thirteen takes to develop the complicated vocal/musical relationship.

The following night, November 1, Jerry Garcia showed up at the recording studio with Jorma and sat in on Marty's frontal at-tack on the technical establishment, "Plastic Fantastic Lover." The song is a bold declaration of war on the straight society of "neon signs," "red tape of mechanical rape" and "IBM." Though Grace did not record that night, she sat in a corner of the control room observing.

The next two sessions, on November 2 and 3, Marty and she recorded "Today" and "White Rabbit" respectively before a week-and-a-half break for rehearsals of the remaining material. The two songs, ironically recorded back-to-back, are reflections of the dichotomy of their sensibilities: differences which were to form the unity and distinctive synthesis of the band. The melan-choly tremor of "Today" is a Keatsian strain updated to San Francisco. Jerry Garcia once again joined in on the third guitar. Grace played an understated piano dominated by the pulse beat of bass and percussion, gently punctuated by the flourishes of guitar. The recording, according to Grace, "went smooth as a goat" and the tracks were laid down in a miraculous one take. Grace's first solo vocal on "White Rabbit" required nineteen different takes. "It wasn't unusual for us to work out a song over and over again. We wanted to get everything right." The lyrics of "Rabbit" had already been heard, when Grace had sung it with the Great Society, but with the sophisticated talents of the Airplane behind her the song reached its musical potential, becoming one of the basic classics in the rock library.

The next song they recorded was Jorma's slightly bizarre "⅗ of a Mile in 10 Seconds." According to Grace, "a lot of times our titles had nothing to do with our lyrics. You'd come up with a title first and try to stick a song on it, or come up with a song and try to stick a title on it, and if you couldn't get the two to match, the hell with it. ⅗ of a mile had something to do with cars. What, I couldn't tell you." The song went down in a surprising two takes.

The days passed around and through these recording sessions. On the afternoons when nothing was scheduled, Paul used to drive over to visit his old friend David Crosby of the Byrds, who was then living in Laurel Canyon. Grace went along for the ride.

In this pastoral setting of calm shepherds lying on grass with their ladies, she entered the high kingdom of the rock underground. Amid hand-carved canoes, wall-to-wall arts and crafts and naked mistresses feasting on natural foods, a mustachioed leonine Crosby reigned over his two or three old ladies in a blissful camelot of free love. When Grace realized that the beautiful blond Anglo-Saxon flower children were all girlfriends of Crosby, "I had to hand it to him, but I couldn't figure out how in the hell he pulled it off."

In these early days of macrobiotic diets, beautiful bronzed bodies and natural juice men, Grace remained somewhat detached from the crowd. In a free-flowing swirl of naked bodies, she kept her jeans on. She walked around the house looking at the arts and crafts as if she were exploring a primitive museum.

Though she remained cautiously detached, she could hear the strains of guitars as Kantner and Crosby serenaded these ladies with sweet harmonies from whatever songs they were then working on. "Nobody ever performed," clarified Grace. "The atmosphere was low-key and free like a modern idyll. We were just opening our heads to human experiences . . ."

On November 14 the band went back to recording and finished up the album in four more days in the studio. The first night went abnormally well with Jerry Garcia and Skip Spence both sitting in on guitars. It started with the chords of "J.P.P. McStep B. Blues"; the song was written by Spence and went down in a lightning two takes but eventually got dropped from the album. The following song, "How Do You Feel," by Tom Mastin, another friend of the band whom Grace had never met, was a re-creation of an acid trip closeted in romantic imagery, the presentation played out through the back and forth of voice and guitars.

The following evening, November 15, Jarrard presided over another thirteen takes to satisfy Grace's perfectionist streak, this time on the recording of "Somebody to Love." The energy level was less intense in the next song, "D.C.B.A.—25" (the title lists the chords of the song), but it was just as much work, another ten takes. The subject of the lyrics is a marijuana high. The next night marked the recording of Marty's ode "Comin' Back to Me," a beautiful dream sequence combining Marty's vocal, Jorma's acoustic guitar and Grace's gentle recorder. Six days later the final cut, and the only instrumental, was laid down, a solo performance by Jorma entitled "Embryonic Journey." Jorma reportedly composed the piece while the rest of the album was being recorded.

Now, with all the tracks safely in the can, it was time for Rick Jarrard to start to perform. In this room full of knobs, gadgets and tapes, Grace watched the engineers at work. With a quick turn of the dials, they changed the tone qualities on the voices and instruments to give them the sound appropriate to whichever track was involved. Through an adjustment of the mechanism, he could make the voices sound more sympathetic and consequently more together in harmonies. "I was knocked out when I heard it," said Grace, "because the guy obviously knew what he was doing." Jarrard tailored the initial tracks into intricate arrangements with tonal shadings which evoked the moods of the songs. Through his turning of knobs and flicking of dials, he translated a fine rock album into a moving work of art.

8

While Rick Jarrard was mixing the album, Jerry Slick was mixing it with Ginger back in Haight-Ashbury. Dark-haired Ginger was one of the unsung heroines of the era. She had grown up in Santa Cruz, one of five kids in a family with little money. After graduation from high school she had become a waitress in several local luncheonettes, and was more into "falling in love and running off than achievement. I was totally escaping any responsibility other than getting high and enjoying myself. I lived in the now." While still a teenager, she married Bill Laudner, a large Olympian surfer who eventually became permanent road manager for Airplane. As a newlywed, she developed a crush on Paul Kantner, who was then a local folk singer. She had eventually left her husband to become the lady of the household for Paul, then for both David Crosby and David Freiberg, who split the grocery bills and shared lady loves.

Through Crosby she eventually became an in-house go-go dancer for the Byrds, playing one-night stands on their cross-country tour. There was also a brief but enlightening stint with the Merry Pranksters at a time when the Hell's Angels were still cramming for their acid tests. When she returned to San Francisco, she struck up a friendship with Bill Graham, who let her into the Fillmore to "get high and dance." There she met Jack Casady and moved in with him. "He didn't want me around that much," she said. "He was only putting up with me. He was always telling me to get a job and move out but I didn't want to work. I wanted to dance . . ."

By the age of twenty-two, the outwardly ebullient Ginger had developed an ulcer from living with a musician who was constantly rejecting her. "He gave me the clap four times. He would come off the road and fuck me, and take me to the doctor the next day. Then he got smarter. He started taking penicillin on the road . . ."

When Grace and Jack left for Los Angeles, Ginger had no illusions about what would go on down south. "I knew Jack thought she was fabulous. He was always talking about how 'incredibly' independent she was. And I knew she and Jerry were breaking up." Since Grace was screwing her old man, she set her own sights on Jerry. At the airport as the band was taxiing off down the runway, Ginger turned to Jerry, asking casually: "Your place or mine?"

"Grace and I were both very aggressive," explains Ginger in the context of the times. "If we wanted a guy we went out and fucked him. We just said 'I want you' and went out and got him. Everybody was fucking everybody else. It was all part of the syndrome and the thing we were all in at the time."

From afar in their colonial house in Palo Alto, Virginia Wing was watching the transformation of her daughter. The phone calls between them became fewer and further between. The dinners were reserved only for holidays and even then often were skipped. Chris Wing hung around the band and talked about becoming a drummer someday. But Grace had distanced herself from her family by canceling out their values through her own life-style.

The expression of this new social order was most vivid at the parties, where an amazing cross section of men and women talked, tripped, ate and screwed without first checking out economic status and social positioning. "I talked to the musicians in the Grateful Dead," Grace said, "but I talked as much to the members of their crew. I was not concerned with how much a guy earned or whether or not he had a degree from an Ivy League school. I was more interested in whether or not he had a droll or sarcastic sense of humor and could communicate his thoughts in an open and exciting way to me."

The different kinds of people who socialized together marked a real departure from the straight society, where few bank presidents ever got it on with the wife of an auto mechanic. "I don't think my father ever went to a party with the guy who worked in the garage," said Grace, "nor did my mother ever go to lunch at the country club with the cleaning lady."

In the underground, society was still open. There was no segregation according to race, sex, salary, jobs or even age. Everybody was equal in the early days. "Even children came to our parties," emphasized Grace. "I can remember Girl and David Freiberg bringing their daughter Jessica, and Mountain Girl and Ken Kesey bringing their daughter Sunshine." In the process of socializing men and women were walking around with and without their clothes, however they felt most comfortable, tripping alone and together in corners, screwing strangers or the husbands and wives of their best friends, or just sitting back and observing. "The point was that we didn't make any big deal about what you were supposed to do and not do." Nor did they try to hide what was going on from the children. "They saw everything around them just like the rest of us. We didn't feel there was any need to protect them because nothing we were doing was violent or obscene. We didn't feel it could hurt us or them to see the way human beings behave naturally. We didn't feel anything we were doing was wrong. We didn't feel guilty."

On the contrary, the openness and honesty was refreshing to Grace and a welcome relief from the starched hypocrisy in the "other" society. "Sex was open and relaxed. The masculine macho thing was not very important. What was important at this time was that each one of us move in the area in which we were most capable and explore the different dimensions of our beings. We were able to get a wider variety of personalities, abilities and behaviors in one room peacefully because we could accept each other's differences and peculiarities."

Still in Los Angeles waiting to hear the playbacks of the album, Grace was spending more and more time with Paul Kantner in Laurel Canyon with the local musicians. There in their woodlands hideaway tucked into the fringe of the winding roads, she encountered "bunches of rock and roll people and their sometime ladies who often changed with the hour. David

Crosby came around with his most constant girl Christine, who was destined to be killed in an auto accident but immortalized by him in the song 'Guinevere.' John Barbata stopped by with his two girlfriends; Neil Young dropped in." But Grace best remembers sitting in a car for hours with Stephen Stills saddened and then lamenting the end of his relationship with Judy Collins.

Spencer was into jazz and innovative music more than folk and consequently during this period headed in a different direction in the Laurel Canyon rock band hideaways. One night as he was eating at the counter of a Hollywood drive-in, he heard that his old friend Frank Zappa was recording around the corner with the Mothers of Invention. He finished his hamburger and conversation with Sally Mann, a beautifully sensual girl friend of the band (destined to make a significant reappearance in a later chapter of Spencer's life), and "hung out at Frank's recording session till about five in the morning cementing a few friendships." The following day he described Frank to Grace in glowing terms of genius. "Watching him record was a real lesson because he was everywhere at once. He always had three or four projects going on. Some guys would be rehearsing something in a booth while he was recording eight bars of something else. He'd be in the booth, out of the booth, playing two or three instruments, running back and forth and just directing, arms flying madly." What was really mind-boggling was that he played every instrument. "If he wanted a certain drum part, he'd just go and pick up the drumsticks and play it."

The image Spencer drew verbally was of the Mad Hatter. Grace recalled an excursion during this period into Zappa's "very unique setup" in Laurel Canyon, which was decorated in wall-to-wall sound equipment. "The place was cluttered with girls who had real long hair sticking way up as if it had frizzed from an electric shock. They were wearing these antique outfits down to their ankles in a style out of the 1920s. It was bizarre but so well put together they pulled it off."

His house was shaded in dark stage lighting with Zappa, who masterminded the whole scene, sitting back like an audience taking in the whole action. "He was the straightest person in the

room," said Grace, "if not in rock and roll, and I was fascinated
by him because he was so off-the-wall and bizarre but he didn't
require drugs to get that way." In fact, Zappa didn't take *anything*, which, in this context and scene, ironically made a freak
out of him. His high came through his overactive imagination.
"He was like a human encyclopedia who'd collect information
like a computer and transmute it into music and poster art."
Grace was knocked out by the originality of the man and knew
someday she would like to connect artistically with him.

Back in the recording studio, Rick Jarrard was playing back
the tapes, greatly impressing Grace, who was then admittedly an
innocent in a room among experienced engineers. "I knew nothing about the technical dimension of recording. It was a total
education to me and I thought *every* version of the song sounded
interesting." Though the musicians had input about the final versions on the recording, the decision ultimately was Jarrard's, who
single-handedly tailored the album for the commercial market.
His major contribution was his ability to soften the cacophony of
the group and improve the textures of the harmonies by blending
their voices together. Kantner disagreed with this approach. He
had long preached his own belief that the distinction of the band
lay in the uncompromising individuality and differences among
the musicians. This conviction clashed with the instincts of the
producer, who edged the sometimes wild lyrics in frames of gentle instrumentals. Kantner and Jarrard sparred and nicked each
other; a few verbal lunges and parries did prove fatal to their
continuing relations, but in this round at least, Jarrard emerged
victorious.

Throughout these playbacks, Grace was impressed with Jarrard because "he obviously knew what he was doing." The guys
continued to malign him despite his apparent competency. They
jousted with him daily. By December, when the band was back
in rehearsals for their live performances, they were already talking about trading him in for another producer. Grace disagreed
in silence but never voiced an opinion. "I guess it wasn't that important to me," she explained. "I figured if they wanted to spend
all their time worrying about this shit that was their business;

but I was a singer and I figured I was supposed to sing and not produce the albums."

The album cost eight thousand dollars to produce (eventually it grossed between seven and eight million dollars). Marty designed the jacket and developed the title from a remark of Jerry Garcia. When asked to describe the songs on the album, he told Marty it was "as surrealistic as a pillow." Marty turned it into *Surrealistic Pillow*, and nobody objected too strenuously except Jarrard, who was grumbling in the background about the lack of professionalism of these crazy hippies so loose that they never did get organized, a looseness which nearly drove him berserk when he tried to get them down to the work. Actually Rick Jarrard was a man of his times; nobody in Los Angeles in December of 1966 was particularly well exposed to the hippies. Down in Hollywood the longhairs were still occasional breezes from the north. "People used to look at us funny when they saw the guys with bandannas wrapped around their long hair. And we did the most to emphasize our differences from straight people." Only around Sunset Strip were their freaky outfits commonplace, since they had plenty of competition for attention from the other off-the-wall characters walking the streets.

Their pictures did appear in the local papers publicizing their engagement, between December 4 and 11, at the Whiskey Au Go Go. On the bill with them was the up-and-coming Peanut Butter Conspiracy (who ended up down-and-out). Though Grace had performed with Airplane already outside San Francisco, the earlier concerts were definitely unmemorable. On October 30 they had played gigs at the University of California at Santa Barbara "with a uselessly fucked up PA system." On the following night, for fifteen hundred dollars, they flew to Des Moines for a quick workout at Grinnell College. Thompson read the itinerary and directed the musicians to the plane and place; but Grace was never able to individualize the towns. "My concentration was always on the performance," she explained, "so I never cared much where it was."

In Los Angeles in her formal debut with Airplane Grace was to prove an anomaly on the rock scene. With her tough delivery and strong voice, she was to emerge at the Whiskey Au Go Go as a major personality. The reaction to her individual style was cool fascination, for her come-on was unprecedented, belying offhand comparisons or quick critical judgments. In a world of music undergoing radical transformation, she seemed to embody and express the elusive and mysterious qualities of electronic instrumentation. "She was a visual symbol," remarked one of the RCA engineers, "of what we were starting to hear."

The Airplane were not the only pioneers. Several bands were entering the field of electronic rock as forefathers of the sound of the underground. Though there was no clear-cut relationship between electronic rock and the revolutionary movement in society, the two became entwined through the efforts of these early bands. They were each identifiable and distinguished from the folk groups by their long hair and funky names like Sopwith Camel, 13th Floor Elevator, Loading Zone and the Electric Prunes. Most were never quite able to get it together enough to make a major statement on the scene. With one foot in the gutter of the underground and one hand in the pocket of the record companies, the majority of musicians found it hard to keep themselves on an even footing while stoned on their path bound for glory. Grace, on the contrary, found the dichotomy perfectly congruent with the straight/hip schism in her own personality. "The hippies were saying and doing things that I had always felt but repressed."

Unlike the run-of-the-mill flower children who settled in Haight-Ashbury as a sanction for rebellion against their parents, Grace saw in the colorful streets and free love relationships realizations of her own inner visions. "As far back as junior high school, it just seemed inconceivable to me to be not attracted to other men after I got married. I could not imagine being not attracted unless I was suddenly to develop a hate men trip or move to an isolated farm in the middle of Kansas. Otherwise, I figured I would keep on being attracted to men as long as I could walk around. When I was in high school, I'd be in love with Frank for six months, then turn on to Harry for a passionate two weeks. That made me realize that I could really enjoy two different men in less than a year and I couldn't see any reason to curtail my natural desires. I just assumed I would probably spend more time with the male I married than with another man but I never thought that monogamy was a natural condition for everyone."

Her conceptual *joie de vivre* got a brief play in college when she was something of a party girl; but after marriage she was not willing to run the risk of the ridicule of the straight society which stroked the puritans and branded the hedonists irresponsible, or worse, adulterous. Through Grace had a strong philosophical integrity, she was essentially cowardly. Consequently, she chose reserve to action and pursued her satisfactions through her fantasies and identification with the characters like Molly Bloom and Justine in literature who lived their lives according to their carnal desires rather than the P.T.A. "Justine was a very bright, self-sufficient woman who was able to attract men both physically and intellectually—and also manipulate them through her own attributes. I would have liked to be as interesting as I thought she was and to have used my powers of seduction to know the variety of men she did."

Emboldened by the ethics of the underground and the support of an open society, Grace began to reshape her destiny upon the stage. It was not that she altered her personality consciously, but rather that through the energy of the music she garnered the confidence to project the hidden dimension and strength of her character. Her image on stage was a stunning embodiment of the zeitgeist. What the audience glimpsed was a living incarnation of Haight-Ashbury, for inlaid in her delivery was the conviction of her lyrics. Grace Slick did not sing as much as she *performed* rock music. Like Mick Jagger and Janis Joplin she assumed a posture toward her songs and became, in performance, the ethos of the music.

By the time the band was playing the Whiskey Au Go Go the word had gone out and through the underground about them. Rock musicians from all over journeyed up to L.A. to hear the "hippie musicians." Generally the two-hour sets went smoothly with Grace bringing down the house with her sultry renditions of "White Rabbit" and the light streams of her recorder. The classic performance of the engagement was executed by Marty. Very high on acid during one performance, he fell off the stage "fixated on a pair of enormous tits in the audience." The L.A. experience ended when Casady got busted in the hotel for his collection of eight-foot-long hookahs and the hashish that went along with them.

On December 19 *Newsweek* delivered the ultimate accolade: a picture of the Airplane in performance at the Fillmore, identified as "the most popular of the groups" making music in San Francisco. "It is a cheerful synthesis of Beatles and blues, folk and country, liberally sprinkled with Indian raga . . . One significant characteristic of the San Francisco songs is their length, often fifteen minutes or longer, ample time to build thunderous climax upon climax . . . within a single number to pass through the land of the blues, the folk, the country and anywhere else free-wheeling invention beckons."

To the executives at RCA the article spelled money. Grace thought it was kind of funny. Nine days later, Casady sprung from the hoosegow, the band was back in performance at the Civic Auditorium in San Francisco with the Beach Boys headlining the bill. Noted Phil Elwood in the San Francisco *Examiner:* "The Jefferson Airplane . . . probed into instrumental and vocal regions with which neither their stage colleagues nor the young audience could comfortably identify . . . Marty Balin wiped out every other singer all night and Grace Slick, the only girl on stage during the evening, has a fascinating sour folk-blues timbre and a crisp percussive bite in her interpretations."

A week later, Leonard Feather reversed the compliment in the Los Angeles *Times* by zapping the entire San Francisco Sound. He gave one of his "wilted Feather Awards" to "all those jazzmen who, searching desperately for a way to sell records, dipped into the teen repertoire and fell flat on their sneakers. Second, to the belly-flop of the year: The forced landing of the Jefferson Airplane (a rock group) at a jazz festival." (He was referring again to their performance at the Monterey Jazz Festival.)

The clinker by the eminent Feather evidenced a controversy at the start of 1967 when Airplane was fast rising as the symbol of the revolution in the music of the day. All writers were on the alert for descriptions of the new music but nobody, including the musicians, was yet sure what the San Francisco Sound was all about. As one reporter for *Life* remarked to his editor two days after the dawning of the new year, "I think the key to the whole movement may be Grace Slick."

9

It was a children's crusade, with hundreds of hippies pouring into Haight-Ashbury to celebrate the first Human Be-In on Saturday, January 14, 1967. Unhooking their knapsacks, they stretched out on the lawns of Golden Gate Park, getting higher and higher as they played guitars, made love and discussed the topics of the day, including whether or not it was possible to get high from the baked inner scrapings of banana peels, and whether the mythical acid factory in Big Sur had been the victim of a surprise bust.

The congregation of twenty thousand flower children who had migrated to San Francisco for the Human Be-In marked a turning point in the development of the counterculture. Previously the movement had been growing up hidden from society; now it was calling attention to itself with radical open-air conventions. Thompson was running around expounding upon the historical significance of the event. Grace was unimpressed. "We had been playing in the park for months. Though they called it a lot of different things like 'Sunday for Love' and 'A Day in the Grass,' it was all the same old stuff." After the musicians played, they often put down their instruments and hung out with the crowd. The Grateful Dead and Charlatans were big on this, but Grace never hung out for too long during these LSD picnics because there were just too many people. "I preferred to go home and read a book. I don't like to talk to ten or fifteen people at once. I get more satisfaction dealing with people one at a time."

By the beginning of January, her marriage was holding together by a string. She had backed off and was admittedly acting sort of weird around Jerry. "He was growing unsure about me and I could feel a kind of reticence in him. It was as if he was afraid of letting down his guard for fear I would step on his head." With only a nodding acquaintance remaining between them, she was left pretty much on her own. "It was the first time I was totally free to do what I wanted, and I would get up to write a song around 4 A.M. or take off in the middle of the night for a hamburger. My only responsibility was to the band."

Back in San Francisco, Jack was living with Ginger again. Both were now on penicillin as was their custom whenever he came back from the road. "Paul and Jorma were avid readers and amusing," Grace said, but she still relegated them to arm's length as friends. Though she and Marty were attracted, they both backed off. "We figured it would be dangerous or something," he said. "Off stage we barely talked." The odd man out was Spencer Dryden, who had already succeeded in alienating the other guys in the band. "They thought he was peculiar," Grace said, "and since he was a man, he had more trouble than I did relating to them because he was so bizarre and different. When I acted extemporaneous, they let it roll off their backs by rationalizing that I was an oddball and a woman; but Spencer's unique personality was something they couldn't deal with. Not long after I joined the group, it was apparent that he was becoming the outcast."

Grace watched him from a distance, initially not paying any more attention to him than to anyone else. "I thought he was kind of funny because he wore strange gold chains and little Western suits; but then I figured it was probably because he had played in strip joints down in L.A. When I first met him, he was desperately trying to make the changeover from his slicked-back fifties hairdo to the long hair of the San Francisco freaks." The guys were unimpressed but Grace thought his "bizarre mind" was fascinating. "He would act normal like the rest of us most of the time. Then suddenly the pitch of his voice would rise and he would start talking like a small elf." The transformation delighted her, "for I have never met a guy uninhibited enough to let out the strange little people that most of us have in our heads."

It was around be-in time in January when the two finally got
together, on the Airplane's first major tour of eight concerts in six
days across the country. On January 8 RCA sponsored a formal
introduction of the group to the New York press. "RCA Victor is
cooperating with enthusiasm, if not comprehension," wrote Richard Goldstein in *The Village Voice*. Though the corporate brass
had made the decision to back the San Francisco Sound, they
were obviously not on the same wavelength. The Jefferson Airplane's New York meeting with the straitlaced media was staged
in the "massively marble" Webster Hall in Greenwich Village,
which, according to Goldstein, looked like "18 Loew's Paradise
Theatres stuck end to end . . . A revolving galaxy of mirror-glass
spins slowly from the ceiling like a psychedelic stalactite. Mauve
and rose panels glow like dancehall embers. The walls ooze with
gilt."

It was, to say the least, an inappropriately glitzy setting to
welcome a bunch of hippies into the music establishment. Grace
recalls images of a smorgasbord of olives, celery, carrots, potato
salad and pastrami, free-flowing alcohol at an open bar and
carved ice figurines. "It was our bar mitzvah." The musicians
stayed stoned.

The purpose of this four-figure shindig was to herald the am-
bassadors of the new wave of rock as the greatest thing since
RCA's own Elvis Presley. To get the message across, the group
played two sets and staged a light show. "They tune up while
oily globules . . . merge and repel," described Goldstein. "All
those waxy colors, and all those jagged shapes look like a fetus
having a very tough time of things."

The critics were uncomfortable with the funky appearance of
the group and their light show on stage. After blasting through
more than an hour of music, the musicians reached into the audience for an impromptu session with the Butterfield Blues Band.
Together they jammed on—and on. The audience thinned. The
reporters returned to their typewriters. The ice figurines melted.

The press conference faded swiftly into memory as the Airplane took off for the Middle West. Somewhere between Chicago and Cleveland Spencer and Grace found each other. While

the bags were being collected in a lobby, the two had slipped into the hotel bar together. When the bus pulled up, they boarded together. Around an hour later Thompson turned around to ask Grace something and nearly jumped out of his seat. Behind him, within heavy breathing distance, Grace and Spencer were locked in a hot and heavy embrace.

For the next few hours Thompson cursed the arrows of Cupid. The moment the bus pulled off into a service area, he accosted Spencer. Out of the listening range of the other musicians, he implored him to lay off Grace. "She's married!" he exclaimed, appealing to Spencer's (waning) morals. It was a false tack, since back in San Francisco Spencer still had a live-in girl friend Christine, as well as a wife and a son in Los Angeles. When propriety didn't cut the mustard, Thompson hit him with the facts of business life. "We've got a good thing going," Spencer recalls him saying. "Don't ruin it for all of us."

Grace was unaware of the behind-the-scenes politics about her sex life. As the bus crept on the long, unending highway from Chicago to Cleveland, Thompson popped Life Savers to calm down as he watched the two of them "acting like kids on an overnight camping trip." They nuzzled, kissed, touched and looked deeply into one another's eyes—a backseat Romeo and Juliet. "It looked promising," admitted Spencer, "and then we didn't screw because we hit Cleveland at six in the morning and we had to play the next day at two." The following evening when they returned to New York, they checked into the City Squire and retired to their separate rooms. Spencer lay in bed for a long time with eyes wide open. Finally Grace sneaked up and joined him.

The next morning, according to Bill Thompson, who took special note, they emerged looking kind of smug, with peculiar grins on their faces. By the time the band flew back to San Francisco, Thompson's fears had become reality. Spencer and Grace were playing romantic overtures inside the band. "Thompson was worried about the relationship developing into a political alliance," Grace said, "and he was right because when a man and a woman get together, they do form a very tight faction."

"But I wasn't looking for a business partner," Spencer said. "I needed a traveling companion."

"Spencer was odd man out in the band and feeling kind of lonely. And I was the only chick and they were finding out that I was sort of odd, too, so it was quite natural that Spencer and I drifted together. It was an attraction of misfits and loners on a long tour."

At the airport Grace's Jerry and Spencer's Christine were there waiting for them. Spencer freaked out from the situation. Grace comforted him. Much to his surprise, she ended up being very strong about the triangles. "She didn't feel any guilt and encouraged me not to," Spencer said. "The way she saw it was existential. This was just the way it was."

The days flowed in and out in a complicated rondo of intertwining relationships; the different romantic themes interlaced, then developed separately only to coincide again. There was no direct confrontation between Grace and Christine, as Christine was unaware of Grace's affair with Spencer. Meanwhile, Jerry bided his time with his own brief encounters. "When it came to Grace and me he was a real gentleman," Spencer said. "He understood how hard it was to maintain a relationship when all of a sudden she was starting to hit the big time all over the country and in the studio. There was not much time for her to relate to anybody except the people she was working with."

The encounters between Grace and Jerry became stilted, formalized and finally detached. One night after rehearsal, she came home with the news that she had taken her own apartment. He yielded to her decision without remark or protest.

Though Jerry was never to reveal his deep feelings to Grace, friends report that for years he was devastated. He never remarried. "A lot of couples don't get along any better than we did," he said, "and if it were up to me we would still be married. I never thought about separating. I was the type who felt you married one woman for life. But Grace wasn't one to stick around when things weren't working." Years later she reflected: "I just wanted to be happy but I didn't want to have to work at it."

Grace now shared the privacy of her new Victorian apartment with Spencer. When he was off with Christine, however. she was left to her own impulses. As Spencer acted out the child in him through the "little gnomes" in his personality, she dressed up in costumes to express the different characters in hers. Occasionally, according to Marty Balin, she would show up at rehearsals in character. "There was her Maid Marian period," he said, and later she was to wear her hair in pigtails and perform on stage in her old girl scout uniform. "When I was living with Jerry I would not always do what I wanted for fear of disorienting or upsetting him." Now, alone for the first time, she would live by the dictates of her imagination. "I didn't care if other people thought I was odd or crazy. That was their problem. It didn't bother me what they were saying about me as long as I could keep doing what I wanted."

Around this time she received an invitation from Palo Alto High School inviting her to her class's tenth reunion. She went to the event with a then toothless and long-haired George Hunter. Hunter brought along a couple of guys from the Charlatans, dressed in their usual Wild Bunch outfits. In the milieu of 1967, when eyebrows were still raised over the length of the Beatles' hair, the sight of this squadron of hippies was almost more than any suburban matron could bear. To dress for the occasion, Grace threw on her buckskin mini-skirt and buccaneer boots, and wrapped a psychedelic scarf around her long hair.

Out of the corner of their eyes the proper alumni shot glances at the intruders but nobody dared confront them directly. Never ones to shrink from a challenge, Grace and the Charlatans grabbed drinks and started to circulate among the young executives and their prim and perfectly poised wives. "Whenever anyone asked us what we did, we told them that we were rock and roll singers," said Grace, "to which they always reacted like a recorded announcement: 'Really, oh how interesting!' Then with the smiles plastered on their faces they'd walk away from us."

After forty-five minutes of performing as token hippies, they split. On the long drive back to San Francisco, Grace's wheels were turning. "There wasn't one person in that room that had gone anywhere. They were stuck. What they saw in us was the possibility of change—what they could become—but they were just too scared to reach out and try."

The escapade confirmed her self-impressions. "It was obvious that they were going nowhere because they had not yet developed any particular awareness of the choices available to them. But then, perhaps the sight of us might have planted a seed. In the mind of just one corporate executive or investment banker, we might have stirred a restlessness that would make him reconsider his alternatives . . ."

As the summer of 1967 fast approached, Grace's consciousness was doing an about-face. A year and a half earlier, when she first took peyote, "I gained a clear perception of who I was not." Now the awareness had expanded into a haphazard and hedonistic philosophy. "I began to sense that the transient nature of events extended far beyond the ego and focused on the recognition that taking oneself seriously was nothing but a cosmic joke. Once you realize how illusory man's concepts of his own importance are, you can no longer take the goals, achievements and pecking order of society seriously. It doesn't make any difference whether you win one of the crowns or sleep on the street: these are all just different costumes on one soul. Assuming that through material achievement you can improve your level in the cosmos is like assuming that a particle of sand can become any more than a particle of sand when it resides in the wall of a sand castle. Anything you happen to collect stays here when you go. There are no armored cars in a funeral procession."

At this point the quickest way to Gracie's spirit was through around nine hundred micrograms of acid. Her flow with the universe was on strong currents of psychedelic drugs, and the routine varied according to her impulses and moods. "I did acid whenever it felt appropriate. It could be five days in a row, then nothing for two weeks. There was nothing particularly consistent about the pattern." She had begun to figure out a way of regulating the intensity of the high so that she could "function at several levels at the same time. With my fingernail I'd scrape a coke-spoon-size flake from a tablet and snort it, the same way you might chip flakes off an aspirin tablet if you wanted a mild dosage." In this way she could be high and still get everything done she needed to do. "It helped keep things in functional perspective."

For Grace the high was "a gift in the hand of a problem—the discovering of what we considered another level of the living process. It wasn't a goal-oriented concept; it was a feeling of hope that we had stumbled upon a means of realizing an evolutionary process. I knew people had bum trips on acid but I just figured I wasn't going to get weird on it; I had a positive sense about it and I didn't worry about being indefinitely confined to an institution. I was very clear and open to seeing the changes of any situation at this time in my life. The resulting highs were amplifications of what was going on inside of me. There was very little negativity in my sense of things at that time.

"I felt that humanity within the next ten to fifty years was going to undergo a swing from the idolization of the material intellect and manifest form to that which is not possessable, not collectible. I felt that we were headed for a move to the intuitive where we would put our feelings foremost and follow lives of trust and the simple word, Love. It was just a feeling within me but I could see it in the flexible discoveries of the people around me. They were moving, as I was, toward a more conscious pattern of existence. We were not probing the phenomenon. We did not really want to explore it intellectually. We were just experiencing it together."

Contrary to what one might expect, the musicians did not trip as a group. "If it happened, fine, but we did not make it a point to do acid together." Each of them had individual acid experiences; what they shared was the knowledge that they had achieved these experiences, although their individual perceptions were all different. The group communion with acid was done largely through humor.

"It was like conversation at a cocktail party in that everybody was more or less trying to be amusing and be amused but it never got beyond that point. When anybody got serious, we half put them down for it. We would avoid things getting too heavy at any level. We thought that if we got too dour about things, we'd become bored and boring. And I, for one, was afraid of boredom. I thought that continuing the search through meditation or endless conversations would result in drudgerous discipline. So I liked to move a lot, collect people and remove them or myself when we'd had enough. I thought we held one of the big keys to enlightenment, but it was really just the frosting on the cake."

That summer the group drove down the coast together for a performance in Monterey. The date they had come to play was the brainchild of John Phillips, of the Mamas and the Papas, and record producer Lou Adler. The Country Fairgrounds Arena had for years been the home of the Monterey Jazz Festival. Now, through the weekend of June 16 to 18, it would play host to a new kind of festival. Thirty or so popular rock acts had come together, in the words of Albert Grossman (then manager for Janis Joplin), to "upgrade people's attitudes about a music and a way of life that we all feel strongly about, and which a large part of the adult and music world still consider as something very special or strange, and not part of the mainstream of American life." The profits from the admission fees (which exceeded half a million dollars) were to be donated to charity. All the acts signed a casual contract waiving their fees. Phillips' and Adler's concept would set the precedent for the open-air pilgrimages which were to peak at Woodstock and eventually survive even the tragedy of Altamont: they were born here at Monterey.

Nearly fifty thousand people showed up at the Monterey Pop Festival, dressed in the unofficial uniforms of their generation: love beads, boots, long flowing granny gowns, faded Levi's, stovepipe hats, flowers and bells. Hair was long, men sporting proud ponytails, women with hair flowing *au natural* below their waists. Most people walked barefoot or in sandals. Around the seven-thousand-seat stadium the strong aroma of incense mixed with that of marijuana; joints and acid tablets were passed from hand to mouth with uninhibited generosity. As Grace strolled around the site where the Airplane would perform on the second

night, she was struck by a strange sense of *déjà vu*. Here just a
few years earlier she had strolled with Jerry Slick on their first
date, listening to the musicians play at the Monterey Jazz Festival. Now she had returned to the very stage, this time as a performer. Around her Otis Redding, Lou Rawls, Jimi Hendrix,
Janis Joplin and Brian Jones ("dressed to the teeth in a red vel-
vet cape") passed to and from the high stage. "I didn't think of
anybody as celebrities. Nobody was really famous. We were just
all doing this 'thing' and all that separated the performers from
the audience was the physical fact of the stage."

On the morning of June 17 the benediction of the rite of music
was delivered by Monterey mayor Minnie Coyle. "When I was
first approached, I was reluctant to let this festival happen," she
conceded. "But I'm very agreeably surprised that this is being
run so well and that everyone is behaving so well." Phil Elwood,
who was covering the event for the San Francisco *Chronicle,*
echoed her sentiments. "There was a feeling of love, comradery,
good fun, without any artificiality."

For Grace the gathering of kindred spirits was the realization
of her beliefs. "Everybody was very pleasant, there weren't any
of the bootlicking corporate toadies hanging around just waiting
to grin at your every word. Nobody was really slick or money-
grubbing. The whole atmosphere was very easy and friendly.
There was no differentiation between people, no gaping at the
performers as if they were from outer space. It was just a bunch
of people hanging out and sharing with each other."

One girl tossed miniature orchids as a halo around the audience when Janis Joplin first stepped on stage. Another handed
out hugs and kisses and slightly wilted daffodils. The small
buildings in the valley of the fairgrounds housed some hot dog
stands, but most contained transplants from Haight-Ashbury:
two-day body tattoo decals, psychedelic art posters, underground
publications, homemade macrobiotic dishes, a computerized
electronic musicmaker, a light show and even a sealed-off meditation center.

"The only difficulties," Mayor Coyle cited, "are relatively

minor. I have been getting calls from residents in Seaside and Pacific Grove [nearby towns] about the loudness of the music. It carries very well on the low air-belt we have."

The music got under way on Friday night in a sharp combustion of human energy. Eric Burdon led off; following his powerful presentation was a more subdued set by Paul Simon and Art Garfunkel. On the following day Ravi Shankar proved pure inspiration, sitting cross-legged on the blankets as he performed his classical ragas, drawing one of the largest crowds through his exotic chants and rhythms. "When Ravi Shankar finished his long afternoon sitar performance," wrote Phil Elwood, "the audience applauded for about five minutes." Shankar reciprocated in kind by tossing a few flowers to them, then taking some encore bows.

Grace shared the general impression about Shankar but found herself more drawn to the violent dimensions of rock as performed by the Who, with their smoke-filled finale climaxed by Peter Townshend dramatically smashing his amplifier with his guitar. These acts of destruction symbolized the rush of energy of the art form. Jimi Hendrix, who executed a back flip on one of the tabs of acid supplied to all the musicians gratis by a local chemist, took it one step further: after what Elwood describes as a "vulgar masturbatory sequence with his guitar," Hendrix finally doused the instrument with lighter fluid and set it on fire. To Grace the theatrical act of destruction by flames was an excellent visual image to accompany the incredible friction and volume of rock and roll.

Grace watched the performance with fascination, spellbound by the violence of the music and performance. To her it was Jimi Hendrix who stole the more than twenty-two-hour marathon of acts; but to the critic of the Los Angeles *Times*, the stars of the second night were Otis Redding and Jefferson Airplane. "The Airplane hit hard with Grace Slick's vocal solos on 'Somebody to Love' and 'White Rabbit,' also working from electronic wizardry on a new number called they said, 'The Ballad of You and Me and Prunella' [sic]." Phil Elwood embellished upon their uniqueness. "The Airplane is one of the few rock groups to have emerged in the last year who understand that the way to avoid the monotony of a hard two or four beat, running forever, is through syncopation. Their bassist, Jack Casady, sets up a furious undercurrent of runs and stop-time accented riffs which keeps the Airplane's sound always changing no matter how straight the front line or lyric sound."

In this raunchy rock world born of leather jackets and pompadours with greasy sideburns, musicians were seldom female, and none of them were yet major personalities on the scene. "Nobody expected Grace Slick to steal the show," observed one of the musicians, "we just figured she would come off as a tough chick, an ornament to soften the hard-driving rhythms." It was *The Village Voice* which transferred her indelible impression upon the audience into print. "Amazing Grace," they wrote, "how sweet the sound . . ."

When she walked on stage, according to *Vogue,* she was as "calm, cool and improbable as a daffodil." Moments later, the improbable daffodil was transformed through the torrential delivery of a siren. Wrote Elwood: "Grace Slick of the Airplane crew has a more sultry voice with more musical quality and less guts than Miss Joplin. She is particularly effective in the contrapuntal second part with Marty Balin's lead voice; often Miss Slick and Balin switch parts, and solo . . . it's an effective team and an excellent band. Miss Slick is also an accomplished composer and musician, and working in the context of the impeccable professionalism of the Jefferson Airplane she has plenty of room to demonstrate her talents."

"Compared to Janis Joplin," Spencer said, "she was on the opposite end of the earth. Janis was rough, earthy and raucous; the embodiment of guts. She had a whiskey voice. Grace emerged on that stage as a temptress, sizzling hot and exciting. She was unctuous and aloof—with a voice like a knife."

Increasing attention followed Grace's performance at Monterey, "but I figured it was just because more people at that one event had heard us perform than in six successive nights at the Avalon Ballroom." Though reactions to her had started mythologizing her into her celebrity, she viewed it cynically. "I get more attention, I suppose," she once cracked, "but that's like if you

had a group of five cows and one pig, you'd look at the pig because he was different. I couldn't take over in this group. Are
you kidding? The Jefferson Airplane is six incredible egos."

As a result of Monterey, and despite Grace's protestations, her
cool, dark beauty and haunted aspect now provoked the contin-
ual epithet of acid queen. Grace watched her image appear and
reappear in the media after the festival. There were pictures in
Vogue, citations in *Esquire* and critical garlands in the New
York *Times.* Grace took it all in with a smirk. "There is a major
personality who emerged at Monterey," she conceded. "Her
name is Janis Joplin."

10

Spencer was busy juggling girl friends. So far no problems had arisen because of their fortuitous geographical arrangement. His wife and son were off in Los Angeles. Christine was his steady girl friend in San Francisco. Grace was his constant traveling companion on the road. "Grace always wanted her own room, though, and that used to bother me a whole lot. But we used to knock on the walls for each other. It was kind of romantic. Finally Thompson came up with the idea what we should get a room together. He figured the band could save money since we always wanted adjoining rooms anyway."

Bill Thompson was the group's road manager, their personal friend and many times their internal and external peacemaker. Bill Graham, who had casually been functioning as a big brother and voice of experience, had evolved into their de facto manager after they fired Matthew Katz. Graham had asked for a contract but the band refused, their experience with Katz having left them uneasy with legal signatures. Graham went ahead and handled their business negotiations on a handshake but the conflicts were implicit from the beginning. "Bill's attitude was to make money," explained Thompson, who acted as the go-between between management and musicians. "He felt you play one place and then move on to the next as fast as you can. He had the feeling that a lot of people shared that it was going to be over in a while so you have to get out there and get it quick." As their concerts began selling out throughout the country, Graham started booking them back-to-back. "He had the band working a lot of shows—maybe forty jobs in a month or two. Weekends. Traveling. Living out of Holiday Inns. Maybe four hundred gigs a year. He was doing a terrific job for the band but they didn't like the pressure. And, they didn't particularly want to go into record stores and sign autographs. If they thought he was full of shit, they'd tell him, which burned Graham, who was working his ass off."

According to Grace: "I liked and still do like Graham. He was different from the rest of us. He was a New Yorker, very wary of the 'too loose' attitude, and he was a salesman. And there he was, stuck with a bunch of self-absorbed hippies. It was hard on him, but he handled it very well. More than anything, the guy moved *fast*."

Now the band was working together for what seemed like twenty-four hours a day. "I agreed with Graham that we should keep on playing when people wanted to see us," Grace said, "and the schedule he set up might have been fine for another band that was after faster, bigger bucks, but we were guarding our questionable sanity by taking an easier stand on the touring issue. Graham couldn't understand why we were finding it so hard to get out and give our guts on stage after four hours of sleep and a switch of time zones, and we couldn't understand why he wanted to make so much money."

Surrealistic Pillow was climbing up the pop charts, and Airplane was whizzing around the concert circuit. As a result, the attraction of convenience between Spencer and Grace now blossomed through proximity into a steady relationship, one way of securing stability within a nomadic life. Spencer summarized: "It was music—and someone to cling to." Spencer's memories flow back to showers together in a sleazy Santa Barbara hotel "which cracked us up because there was a seat underneath the shower nozzle. And a bed afterward with lots of fleas . . . Grace was a very energetic lover." There were late-night readings of Terry Southern's *The Magic Christian*. Shared appreciations of the wisecracks of Lenny Bruce. Listenings to Miles Davis and Gil Evans. Arrangements of Grace's songs—she had written "rejoyce" on the piano and Spencer scored horns for it.

"Grace was very unconventional in her attitudes about romantic attachments," Spencer said. "She never got jealous." She couldn't have cared less about his wife and child. "She wasn't even jealous of Christine. She just said, fuck it. Forget the guilt and possessiveness. What is, is."

Christine had a more typical reaction. "We started getting into these terrible arguments about me going on the road," Spencer said. "I tried to keep it like it wasn't happening between Grace and me. But Christine knew and I finally had to make a decision."

As Christine was laying claim to him, Spencer kept right on seeing Grace in San Francisco on the sly. "We used to meet in Golden Gate Park," he recalled. "It was nothing outrageous or anything. We just wanted to be together." On sunny afternoons when Christine was out of the picture for an hour or two, they'd drive up above Larkspur (in Marin County) to picnic. When Spencer went to buy his camper, "which Grace called our little house on wheels," Grace—not Christine—went with him. Spencer, in turn, drove Grace to the Chevy lot, where she purchased a white Corvair. "She used to pooh-pooh everyone in the band for their foreign cars," he said. Picking up on the philosophy of Ivan Wing, "she used to tell me that she would take an American car any day—drive it till it breaks, then go out and find parts for it." (Several years later, in an apocryphal encounter, she walked into an automobile showroom on Van Ness armed with her publishing royalties. On the spot she bought an Aston Martin which caught her fancy for $18,500—in cash.)

He called her Grooch. She tagged him Dopey. As Christine drifted back to Haight-Ashbury, their intimacy tightened.

Surrealistic Pillow had made the *Billboard* charts in March, and it would hit the number 3 slot before settling for the long haul between numbers 10 and 15. It remained on the charts altogether for fifty-six weeks. The biggest thing to happen in rock music in the summer of '67 was the release of the Beatles' "*Sergeant Pepper's Lonely Hearts Club Band.* It was accepted as the first "concept" rock album, and it marked a final jump by the Beatles into pure studio recording, the making of elaborate music which simply could not be duplicated on the concert stage. On a visit to San Francisco that summer Paul McCartney dropped in at an Airplane rehearsal at the Fillmore, joining the musicians during a break for a little DMT (a fast rush chemical related to plastic, familiarly described as "coffee break acid"). "It was so strong," recalled Thompson, "you could take one toke and be off in another zone." McCartney hung out for a while smoking and rapping with the band, then went back to the apartment of Marty, Jack and Bill. "He mostly hung out with Jack," said Spencer, "because they were both bass players and the common instruments became a bond for friendship."

McCartney's curiosity was like everybody else's. The attraction of the Jefferson Airplane was its lyrics. "In a way we were like a musical press," Grace said. "We wrote lyrics out of our experiences." As a result, what they sang rang true, and began raising a controversy. As Grace told *Time* magazine for an article published on June 23, 1967, the lyrics of the songs are "all the same. They say, 'Be free—free in love, free in sex.'" And free in drug experimentation as well, as everyone who listened to the lyrics of "White Rabbit" was sure to find out.

RCA had originally bypassed both "Somebody to Love" and "White Rabbit" to select the mellow cut "My Best Friend" sung by Marty as the single off the album. It was, incidentally and tellingly, probably the least controversial and inspired song on the album. It rose to number 86 on the *Billboard* pop charts then disappeared. In the meantime reviewers of the album gently began to probe the company to hold a second hearing. "The Airplane's popularity comes not from what they say," wrote *Time* in their record review of July 5, "but how they say it: their artful musical ellipses, the easy blend of voices and instruments, and above all the singing of newcomer Grace Slick. Grace controls the sound with dramatic urgency in 'White Rabbit,' her own song about the wonder drugs of Alice's Wonderland ('Feed your head! Feed your head!') and her fervent evangelism for a more universal proposition: 'Don't you want somebody to love?'" Echoed Jann Wenner in his review published in Sunday *Ramparts:* "My favorite track (on the album) is 'Somebody to Love' . . . It should be their next single release." Confirmed John Goodman in *The New Leader:* her rich contralto "can blend or dominate as the situation demands, twist words, bend notes or sing bel canto."

Though a little slow to respond, the recording executives eventually picked the right songs and things began to happen. By April 1 "Somebody to Love" had already made its mark on the *Billboard* charts at number 31. It remained for the next fifteen weeks and reached a high of number 5. Two months later, on June 24, "White Rabbit" also climbed on board and achieved a rank of 8, lingering on the charts for ten strong weeks. Grace was not particularly impressed by her own achievements in this respect, "largely because I didn't know about them. I didn't sit around reading the pop charts so I had no idea I was even on them. Since my radio was broken, I didn't listen to AM or FM so I never heard how much they were playing the songs. I was not especially interested in how important I was supposed to be because I was not impressed by any pop singers including me."

Fortunately the media was not as blasé as she. Through the pages of *Time, Newsweek, Life* and *Look* Grace Slick was made into an overnight phenomenon. Up to this point Marty Balin had been the focal point of Jefferson Airplane. He had sung the lead vocals on five songs on *Surrealistic Pillow* and garnered glowing reviews from the critics. Now it was Grace who was the center of attention. The Airplane was pegged as the leading exponent of acid rock—which was what the San Francisco Sound had finally become—and Grace became its first lady. The term acid rock was even then a slippery one: it didn't mean that the musicians would perform while tripping, because the acid would make it impossible to perform professionally without overwhelming internal distractions. Nor did acid rock mean that the listener had to be tripping to appreciate it (although not infrequently this was the case). What it finally came out as was that acid rock was the occasionally far-out experimental rock where both the performers and audience were a part of the drug scene, and the music resultingly "druggy", even if nobody happened to be stoned at the time. To be a fan of acid rock you never had to touch a drug in your life. But it helped.

Whether or not they played on acid was obviously not the

point: their lyrics were filled with references to their trips. With Grace's own "White Rabbit" widely acknowledged as the classic of the genre, it was hardly surprising that she would become one of the leading composers and voices on the scene. Besides, in and around Haight-Ashbury, the notorious chemist Augustus Owsley, the Johnny Appleseed of the psychedelic explosion whose concoctions would come out in batches with names like sunshine, white lightning and baby Jesus, delivered generous supplies backstage to them gratis. The band had an arsenal of drugs that would be the envy of any mind-altering researcher. "They were like the nouveau riche," said Jerry Slick; "they only had the finest kind."

This recognition of these bands as the kingpins of the drug culture flourishing in San Francisco was widespread among the hip generation. So it was only natural once Grace was anointed by the media as the first lady of hard rock that she would also bear the title, by inference, of acid queen; it was the thrill of this image coupled with the intriguing lyrics of "White Rabbit" that catapulted her to an unprecedented status and edged Marty Balin out of the spotlight.

Off the record Grace was amused by the epithet, since there were "probably fifty or a hundred girls around who took eight times more acid than I did; but I wrote about it and wasn't afraid to speak about it so they nailed me as the acid queen."

The coronation came when the group first sang on "The Smothers Brothers Comedy Hour" in 1967. "Right after Grace did 'Somebody to Love,' everybody started yelling for 'White Rabbit.' They wanted Grace Slick and they started screaming for Gracie," Thompson recalled. Parenthetically, the camera did not even focus on Marty, who was behind her during the performance of her song playing tambourine.

In the days that followed Bill Thompson noted the changes: "Marty withdrew into a shell, a total shell." Contrary to the obvious assumption, however, Marty did not have major problems with Grace's fame. "I realized by then that if you put no importance on fame, it was just a passing show," Marty said. "At first, in the early days of the band, it really bothered me when everyone knew me on the street. They began treating me special and I didn't like it."

In the beginning of the shift in power within the band, there were twinges for him. "But after I got past it I began to appreciate the fact that she took the brunt of all the publicity. She loved it and it took the pressure which I had dreaded off me. It gave me a chance to produce without hassles and not have to become somebody bigger than life. I didn't have to be anybody except myself. And I'm essentially a loner and invisible man."

Behind the scenes of the band, another more complex drama was taking place. Jack and Jorma were growing more and more discontented playing Marty's romantic ballads and listening to what they thought was his ultra-sweet crooning. One night Jack confronted Marty with their sharp criticism of his songs. They wanted him to write more relevant material. They called his lyrics corny and disgustingly sentimental. Though he showed no emotion on the spot, Marty was not to rebound easily from the blow to his ego. His lyrics were a baring of his soul. Vulnerable to the point of fragility, he withdrew quietly without flap or reference to the hostility building as a defense inside of him. He voiced no complaints, and never discussed the criticism with anyone. "But," Thompson noted, "on the next album he contributed barely a half of one song."

11

They had the number 3 album in the country that summer and Graham had them booked for concerts from coast to coast without a break. On the road in the fall of 1967, the band was in the midst of completing their next album, and exhausted. At this point, during a meeting in a hotel room, Graham told the group that he had decided to extend the tour. Spencer jumped up and exploded. In front of the rest of the band, he shouted: "Bill, your brain is made of money!"

The room fell silent. Graham stood still "and fixed this stare on me," Spencer recalled, "then he vowed he'd never forget what I had just said. I accused him of putting money before the art, and Marty chimed in by telling him that he didn't care *how* long it took to do the next album. Marty didn't see any reason to go in there and cut something just for the sake of getting an album on the shelves. He didn't want to be locked into a syndrome where we'd have to make a record and then support it by touring. He wanted us to take an entire year to turn out what he thought would be a real tasty product which we would want to support."

Grace watched the power play in silence. She didn't want the obviously unpleasant tempers turning on her. Besides, she was enough of a politician to let Spencer do her dirty work and to keep her own status non-partisan. As a result, nobody ever put the finger on her but instead they bore the grudge against Spencer, whom they figured was manipulating her power in the group to his advantage.

"They were right about it," she said, "and wrong, too. I agreed with Spencer about Bill Graham working us too hard, but disagreed on the way it was handled. We could have worked out a compromise with him if we had come on differently." None of the band were diplomats, however, and Graham would often fly out of hand when his authority was openly thwarted. Their meetings were more often battles of wills than symposia of opinions or open dialogues.

Behind the scenes, Spencer and Grace would share observations about the band. "The whole thing was getting out of hand," Spencer said, "and we were both unhappy about it." Alone, they would talk about how good it could be. "'If only Paul would practice more and Jorma would not cut himself off from the others with Jack.' 'If only Marty would contribute more again and everybody would go along with one idea . . .' We talked about the problems of making music with friends," Spencer said, "and how none of the others understood me. Everybody was such an individual that they would never listen to each other. We'd be playing one tune and it was like playing six arrangements in each song because everybody would keep musically insisting on their own way. There was no give-and-take, no working together, and it was all getting to be chaos rather than music-making. Grace and I couldn't do the kind of thing we wanted. And Jorma and Jack felt the same way. Marty had all but withdrawn creatively, and only Paul was left, trying to hold the thing together."

"Paul was like the camp counselor," Grace said, "trying to get all the kids to one activity."

The only thing any of the Airplane really wanted was to make music. Unfortunately, the recording of their next album was wedged in between gigs without a creative break. "We felt we had to come up with a hit," Spencer said; "we had to go in there and produce whether or not the inspiration was with us."

As the pressures intensified, the band became more and more rebellious. "In a way it was us against Graham," Grace said. "He was determined to teach us how to be more professional and we were just as determined to teach him how to loosen up." During a concert with the Grateful Dead at O'Keefe Center in Toronto, Marty encouraged the entire audience to get up and dance as in the festivals in San Francisco. "The place went crazy," Thompson observed. "Maybe three or four thousand people stood up in the aisles and started moving to the music. This kind of thing had never happened there before and it blew the minds of the security police, who kept telling Graham the band was responsible if somebody got killed." Though Graham laid the law down to the group afterward, none of them were apparently listening to him. That night in the halls of the sedate Royal York Hotel, Airplane and Dead got together in one of the rooms and jammed and smoked dope. The fumes scented the hallways and Graham was sure some businessman would report them and they would be busted. "Graham didn't smoke grass," Thompson noted; "he frowned on it."

Still, Graham was a strong-willed businessman and not yet discouraged enough to give up. According to Grace: "We sort of felt like a bunch of freaked-out juvenile delinquents with this Spencer Tracy character ever hopeful of our improvement."

So rock and roll was becoming a paradox. On the one hand, Airplane were the foremost music-makers in San Francisco, but fame ironically was giving them less and less time for songwriting and recording. As the business grew so did the complexity of the operation; the chaos and sense of confusion, disguised heroically in their relentless experimentation, were sadly reflected in their next album.

The success of *Surrealistic Pillow* had given them the clout to get artistic control in their contract. As a result, they nixed the return of Rick Jarrard and rejected his replacement, "a slick, swarthy type," recalled Thompson, "with a big cigar in his mouth. His big thing was that he had produced the song 'I Left My Heart in San Francisco' and he told you about it all the time."

The producer finally chosen was former engineer Al Schmitt. Thompson recalls that the first time Schmitt walked into the Fillmore Auditorium "he saw Graham throwing chairs around the place because he was so angry. The group, per usual, wouldn't do something he wanted them to do." Thus Schmitt got his first dose of the scene. He spent time rapping with the musicians, who, except for Grace, "did not like the sound of *Surrealistic Pil-*

low because there was far too much echo on it," Schmitt said. "They made it clear that they had not been happy with Rick Jarrard." Schmitt took the cue and henceforth basically took his direction in the studio from them.

"Al Schmitt was very easygoing around us," Grace said. "He wasn't put off by our insanity. He was open and flexible. There was a rapport without our being conscious of the differences between us. He was a lot closer to playing the game, although he was still out of the straight world. But there was less of a polarity between us and he was open to our interest in experimentation."

The creation of *After Bathing at Baxter's* took nearly six months in a series of madcap segments in the studios in Los Angeles. By this time, RCA had just about given up on trying to reform these musicians. Though they broke every rule for recording in the studio, *Surrealistic Pillow* had earned enough money for the corporation to let them get away with it. Unlike most groups, Airplane walked into the recording studios, where the tab was around one hundred dollars an hour, with absolutely no idea of what they were going to do. Grace, however, was an exception to this rule. Though impulsive to the brink of lunacy when goofing off, when it came to songwriting she was compulsively organized. In a small black notebook she would work out the lyrics in rushes of creativity. "The source of a lyric could be anything taken from anywhere, an overheard phrase, a billboard slogan. Once an idea would get into my head it would work its way around on its own time and eventually come out, maybe an hour later, maybe a year later, sometimes almost in finished form at the start, sometimes needing reworking over a long period of time."

What distinguishes her two songs on this album is their literary bent. "You don't dance to her songs," Ralph Gleason once remarked in passing, "you sit down and take notes for English 101." She recorded "Two Heads," her first song for the album, on June 28, its source a cartoon illustration in a book of Spencer's. "It was an anti-WASP, anti-alcoholic, anti-war, anti-frigid, anti-middle-class-morals song against the suppression of the free soul inherent in every individual." In "rejoyce," recorded three months after "Two Heads" on September 22, 1967, she produced a classic, and, in the words of *Newsweek*, one of the most "brilliant" songs in the Schwann catalogue, a four-minute pastiche of James Joyce's *Ulysses* updated for the modern generation. "Some of 'rejoyce' was taken from Molly Bloom's soliloquy, some of it was from Stephen Dedalus and some of it from Bloom. It was the same three hunks the book was written in. Joyce was making a statement about the middle class in the book, and I was simply touching one side of its relevancy."

The recording sessions were the first of their kind in the history of the RCA studios. "They recorded the album by trial and error," said Al Schmitt. "They really wanted to experiment with new dimensions of sound." Each musician worked separately. For instance, Jorma, Schmitt recalled, "would play long sustaining notes and hold them to create a blended line. Grace picked up on this vocally" and in these sessions began to imitate his techniques on the guitar with her voice. "She would turn her head from left to right to create weird but interesting nasal noises. On other days, she would keep changing her position from left to right in front of the microphone to see what changes she could create in her own tonalities."

"Unfortunately," Grace said, "we were trying to become Einstein without ever having studied physics. We wanted to discover new dimensions of sounds and ways to work with complex instrumentation but we had no idea what we were doing. So we'd move around amps and mikes to see what changes the different positioning created for us. We tried an awful lot of things to find out what we could do with the different electronics. We were more interested in the sounds and special effects on the album than in coming up with familiar and popular tracks. We figured we were going to produce the most brilliant album ever released in the field of rock. Instead what we came up with was probably the most obscure and chaotic one."

The sessions in the recording studio were spread over a hectic period of four months. During this time the band rented a

Beatles throwaway mansion in Beverly Hills for an exorbitant
five thousand dollars a month. There the group reclined in splen-
dor amid automatic waterfalls and pleasure gardens. It was small
wonder that not much work was really done. The tracks for the
first song, entitled "The Ballad of You & Me & Pooneil," were
laid down on June 26, and the final song, entitled "Spare
Chaynge," was finished up on October 31, less than a month before the album was officially released. "It was among the first
albums in this country recorded on eight tracks, and the lyrics
were incredible," said Bill Thompson, voicing the excitement of
the band. "It was one of our most creative albums," Paul confirmed, "but it wasn't produced well because we produced it
ourselves and we didn't know how."

Five songs plus one collaboration, the majority of the album,
were composed by Paul Kantner. The result was a reflection of
his preferences, according to Grace, "for around 90 per cent harmonies and loose improvisations." His approach to arrangements
was just the opposite of hers because "Paul likes to leave things
up to the individuals. He feels that the diverse styles of the musicians were the earmark of the band which should develop or-
ganically as we recorded his songs. He encouraged improvisations and changes."

His songs on this album employed the three-part harmonies of
Grace, Marty and Paul, punctuated with impulsive counterpoints
and changes of rhythm. Because Paul was open to spontaneity
Grace was free to develop the background improvisations which
were to become the essence of her style. The more she took off
vocally, the more resentful of her intrusions was Marty. He
openly disliked her vocal impulses, which he felt distorted the
natural flow of the harmonies. "She'll turn around and not give a
shit about what something sounds like and destroy a song by
singing all over the place," he explained. "A song has a certain
energy, a certain form. I think you should first understand form
before you break it up." Grace was unaware of his resentment,
though the rest of the musicians were concerned by it. "I always
figured it was all right with Marty," she said, "because he never

said anything to me. Sometimes he seemed upset or discouraged but how did I know that I was causing it? He just withdrew into his shell."

Improvisations were the key to her impulsive character and rapport with the other musicians but "when she follows her own impulses," points out Marty, "she does away with the natural phrasing of the songs. Grace never was sensitive to what her singing was doing to the other musicians. She was all wrapped up in what *she* was doing."

Grace expected the other musicians to react instrumentally to her stimulus. "The thing I like best about a rock band," she once said, "is that you never know what is going to happen next. One person does something and another reacts. It is total improvisation, which means that things can never get boring." Throughout the making of *After Bathing at Baxter's* Grace was striving to expand her range. "Since I had never taken a singing lesson I didn't do it properly by exercising vocally," she said. "It was trial and error all the way." For the first time in her life, Grace had encountered a situation where she was being paid to follow her own impulses which had previously set her apart from most people. In the recording studio she was discovering a "state of joyous confusion which was feeding my head with the experiments of other musicians as off-the-wall as myself. It was a time of discovery and creative freedom." And, Thompson added, "we were pretty sure what we were doing would become the greatest album ever."

One of *Baxter's* distinctions—and possible later reasons for its disorganized form—was the number of would-be musicians who contributed their ideas to the compositions. Besides Thompson and his boyhood friends, who were developing into an extended family of the band, there were other friends and groupies also hanging out. What frankly delighted Grace about this crew was the variety of people. "At the time we were obviously not isolated by this star thing," she said, "we just were hanging out with our friends."

Naturally the extended family gloried in the reflected limelight and edged as far into it as the musicians would permit. Thompson appointed his friend Gary Blackman as artistic director of the company and together they searched for a title for the album through his pages of unpublished poems, finally suggesting *After Bathing at Baxter's*. Together Thompson and Blackman were also composing with Spencer and came up with a song in dialogue entitled "A Small Package of Value Will Come to You, Shortly." It was a cacophonous rumble akin to the street scenes in *West Side Story*. To record it, the band rented a box of sound effects from one of the movie studios and the three stooges sat in a corner putting together an atonal score of cowbells, bongos, mumbling, piano, shouts, and xylophone tones capped off by Blackman's recitation of John Donne's "No man is an island" to which Thompson replied: "He's a peninsula."

This offbeat humor was to define all the recording sessions, during which Jorma used to ride his motorcycle through the studio while waiting around for Jack to lay down his tracks. "It was a big studio," Grace said, "so nobody paid much attention." When one journalist asked Jorma why he was doing it, he replied, "Why not?"

"It could take three or four hours for Jack to finish up," said Grace, "because like the rest of us he was experimenting with the way the position of the mikes, amps and different gadgets for his instruments affected and changed the tones. Since we didn't want to follow a schedule or regiment each other in any way, the rest of us couldn't go off because we never knew when he would finish and it would be our turn."

From the control room, Schmitt took all this in good-natured stride. "He chose to accept it rather than climbing up a wall," Grace observed. "He'd just laugh at what was going on and gently try to get us back on the right track to get the album done."

By November 27, 1967, RCA had packaged this very odd assortment of eleven songs into an album. "*After Bathing at Baxter's* was pure LSD, among thirteen other things," said Paul Kantner, "and the recording executives just didn't know what to make of it." By this time, they were hesitant to censor anything the Airplane did so they went ahead and marketed the album without trying to change it. The record was divided into five movements entitled "Street Masse," "The War Is Over," "Hymn to an Older Generation," "How Suite It Is" and "Shizoforest Love Suite," which had nothing to do with the songs but were rather bits and pieces of inspiration deliberately undeveloped. "If it were up to Spencer, me and Thompson, it would have been all bits and pieces," said Grace. "We liked to put together things that we thought were interesting, without particularly bothering to connect them." The concept as an album was bombastic and overblown in impulsive artistic pretensions. Though the songs were at times interesting explorations in electronic sound and vocal ranges, the temperament of the album was chaotic and whimsical.

Commercially the album failed to prove arresting. Though RCA printed 325,000 copies in advance (72,000 were ordered for the San Francisco area alone), the album did not live up to its potential. It hung on the Billboard charts for twenty-three weeks but never moved up past the seventeenth position. The failure was to cause more conflicts with Bill Graham, who began to come down hard on them to produce another commercial album like *Surrealistic Pillow*. "He wanted us to write more songs that you could whistle," said Paul. "He wanted us to be seriously commercial."

Their occasional pranks annoyed Graham but the commercial disappointment fired him up. Tensions continued to increase as he kept pressuring them to write more commercial songs and perform more and more concerts on tour. At the meeting at the end of December, Spencer demanded that Graham supply them with a bottle of Southern Comfort at every gig. "Graham flipped out about it," said Thompson. "He thought the bottle of Southern Comfort was the most outrageous thing in the world, despite the fact that when they were playing at the Spectrum the Grateful Dead threw their plates of spaghetti on the promoter's head because he didn't get them steak for dinner."

"I thought it was disgusting," observed Marty after the scene. "They made demands on Graham and wanted to be treated like great stars. At the time I didn't have the authority to stop them because Grace was the one with the two hits in the band."

"Everybody wanted Grace," said Spencer. "It was like dating Marilyn Monroe, but she wasn't happy about what was going on. Because we were together I think she would verbalize it in private just to me. She felt it was turning into a business and used to say it's not as much fun as it should be. And she wasn't thrilled by the fact that everybody [since the publication of the *Look* magazine article the previous spring] was calling her 'Gracie.'"

Spencer became her mouthpiece and *de facto* manager, expressing her opinions while she remained behind him in silence. "There were times when I'd say to the band, 'if you guys don't straighten up and get something together musically, Grace and I are going to form our own band.'" Neither Spencer nor Grace was signed to the contract with RCA since they had come into the band as replacements. "So we used it as a lever against RCA and the other musicians.

"The final straw to me was when Graham suggested we use the Geary Temple for rehearsals," said Spencer, "then tried to charge us for it." The conflicts reached that pitch after Graham now presented them with a contract. "He wanted 15 per cent. I said nobody gets 15 per cent. He said that Albert Grossman was taking 50 per cent of what Janis made. I told him that Grossman was a shmuck."

On an afternoon in January 1968, Spencer laid down the ultimatum: either Graham or Grace. If the band did not get rid of Bill Graham, he and Grace would sign a contract with another recording company. At this point Bill Thompson stepped in as henchman. He made a round of phone calls to find out how RCA felt about dropping Graham as the manager. "I also called Chuck Seton, our attorney in New York, to find out if he would still continue to represent us, and I called Bill Coblentz, who is a highly respected attorney in San Francisco. They both said they would stay on."

With these assurances, "Marty and I went [over to the Fillmore] to fire Bill Graham. We just told Bill that Grace was not going to continue to perform under these circumstances. I'll never forget; his face just turned white." Later, he called Thompson up at home. "He thought I'd put a knife in his back, and raised holy hell with me. When I hung up all I could think was, 'Holy shit. What is this? Rock and roll or a horror movie?'"

12

Grace and Spencer moved into an old San Francisco building on Washington Street, one flight down from Jorma and his wife Margaretta. "It sure took her long enough," Spencer said. "I was really happy in my apartment on Franklin Street," Grace explained. "I didn't want to give it up because I was pretty sure it was better than the situation I was moving into."

They were, however, spending all their time together and "it was natural to live together. There was no big commitment or effort. It was just the right thing to do at the time." They had been looking for a place for quite a while when Jorma told Spencer that an apartment in his building was vacant. What sold Grace on it was the fact that it had two bedrooms. Before she agreed to live with Spencer, she wanted to make sure she had a room of her own—"just a space where I could throw all my junk, guitar, piano and drawing materials as well as my television set which I had yet to turn on. I could be with Spencer twenty-three hours a day but I needed at least one hour to be by myself. I never thought my intense need to be alone was particularly unusual, and without my own room as an escape hatch, no relationship I could have could ever possibly work. I had read somewhere that Daniel Webster had had nine children, and got his own room in the house soundproofed. I identified with that, at least the room part."

The steady income from the group allowed her to buy whatever she wanted, which meant an eclectic assortment of objects reflecting her own unusual tastes. If she saw something she liked, she'd buy it, sometimes to the dismay of Spencer. "She just loved to throw it away," he said. "I don't know how many arguments

we had about money." Her first major purchase for their new living room was an antique wood wheelchair, "which was highly
practical. I put it by the fireplace as an armchair and since it was
on wheels I could move it around, too." Alongside was a Louis
XV brocade love seat with a carved hood and mysterious
pockets. On the walls she hung Spencer's surrealistic pencil
drawings, a collage of Barry Goldwater eating a plateful of
Lenny Bruce, psychedelic posters from the Fillmore and a
couple of paisley shawls.

Meanwhile, her relationship with Spencer was proving fragile.
"Spencer had a great capacity for intimacy. He could be kind,
gentle, giving and responsive. He would ask me why I was acting screwy when I didn't know I was acting screwy. He was
more in touch with my feelings than I was and he would just
keep asking me what I was feeling until I could see it myself. He
could pull teeth gently." Though his sensitivity had initially appealed to her, as the weeks went on he became more than she
had bargained for in this respect. "I was twenty-seven years old
but not yet ready to assume responsibilities. I was only playing
at being a grown-up and as long as we were playing games the
relationship was fine with me; but Spencer was having serious
problems with the band, which had a strong effect on him. He
was more intense than the other guys in the group, and they
would make fun of him and abuse him and he started doing
speed and alcohol out of self-defense."

Spencer's problem was that he couldn't handle the amount of
drugs he was doing, and Grace's problem was handling him
when he couldn't get out of bed in the morning. "I'd say:
'Spencer, it's time to get up.' And he'd say: 'Five more minutes.'
And I'd say: 'Spencer, we have to catch a plane.' And he'd say:
'Can't I make the next flight?'

"He was having a real tough time and I was not committed
enough to help him through it. All I saw was a person going half
crazy and I knew I couldn't handle writing music, singing and
the friction that was developing between the band members and
Spencer. He was acting weird and I was his go-between. But I
just couldn't nurse him."

The relationship disintegrated slowly because "I was too chickenshit to say to him: 'Hey, I like you as a friend but this isn't working out between us living together.' It was kind of incongruous being this so-called symbol of free love yet not having the guts to end this relationship." What she did eventually was to rent a place of her own in Sausalito. "I told him that I thought we should have a country house, but he wasn't stupid."

She started spending more and more time in Sausalito with Jerry Slick coming around. Spencer began entertaining groupies in between Grace's frequent trips into his bedroom. "We didn't want to be together all the time, but we didn't want to give each other up yet either."

With the passing of Bill Graham, the band was left without a manager, and Bill Thompson, who was everybody's friend, took the reins. Grace had serious reservations about having a hippie direct the band. "I thought we should get a shyster from New York or Los Angeles—or at least somebody who could add." Thompson, however, had served his apprenticeship as confidant and go-between with Graham as road manager. Plus, he had the strong support of Paul. "I didn't want to create any more friction in the group," said Grace, so once again her judgment went unvoiced.

The situation with the group was a bold contradiction of her determination to see rock and roll as a constant amusement. The tensions between the musicians and the verbal abuses against Spencer were downright unpleasant, and this combined with her failing relationship and her inability to extricate herself from it. Then too, there was her singing. She had no formal training, and the strain of shouting through concerts to be heard over the amplified instruments was ruining her voice. "I'd be going for one note and hitting another. It was a real embarrassment in front of thousands of people. To cover up, I'd do something crazy on stage so the audience would think I was only clowning around. I didn't know what was happening to my voice: it sure wasn't going in the direction of the song."

As her protector, Spencer blamed it on the band and the heavy schedule of concerts. He used it as a lever to slow down the touring. Marty convinced Grace to try singing lessons, but the instructor had no experience in rock and wasn't really helpful. Finally she got the condition diagnosed and checked into a hospital in Berkeley to have a node removed from her vocal cords (she was subsequently to have two more of these operations). "I wasn't worried at all since I had read that Harry Belafonte had gone through the same operation nine different times."

Finally, there was Grace's drinking. "The problems with the group didn't start me drinking—I'd been doing that since I was fifteen. I was born crazy. Alcoholics Anonymous defines an alcoholic as a person who has lost the ability to control his drinking. I never *wanted* to control my drinking; I'd get drunk specifically because I wanted to throw away all my controls, to let go of everything. I was never a social drinker, a couple of glasses of wine here and there; I drank to get *drunk*. It was periodic, every week or every few weeks, and when it happened it was completely loony tunes. I was under the delusion that there were a whole bunch of people out there just as screwy as I was, but I was wrong. Nobody, except maybe a few other alcoholics, went to this extent with it, were this violent about it. And the ambience of a rock and roll group at that time, with its up-front anti-society position, combined with the basic craziness of rock in general, provided a scene that supported me in this. The individual members of the band didn't want to see me go crazy—far from it—but the situation was there, and none of us had any control over it."

The dark side of Grace now was emerging at odd intervals on the road. On alcohol her natural reserve and defensive antagonism were transformed into sarcastic exhibitionism. In the beginning of the band her crusades were direct, but as her drinking increased, her assaults grew more creative and insidious. In the redneck section of Bakersfield, California, where Buck Owens and Merle Haggard were still considered raunchy, Airplane jammed for over three hours in concert and the police turned off the stage lights because they felt the performance had gone on long enough. In the darkness Grace and Paul continued playing and led the audience in a sympathetic chant that went: "Fat pig, fat pig!" As a result, Airplane was banned from Bakersfield by a dictate of the chief of police. There were roller skating derbies with road manager Bill Laudner through the Los Angeles airport and a bare-breasted performance in Gallic Park when during a light drizzle in an outdoor concert she took off her shirt, explaining to the audience: "I don't want to get it wet." While the other musicians argued with the stage crew about putting on a light show during their numbers on "The Smothers Brothers Comedy Hour," Grace went into the make-up room and came out with a black face. "Nobody said a word to me, so I went on camera and sang 'White Rabbit' that way."

Ironically, her daring against convention, minor pranks in the midst of the total social revolution, were having their effect. Her violation of convention was turning on the very straight people she was putting down. The invitations and praises from highbrow cultural mavins came pouring in. "They wanted to pay us a lot of money [as much as ten thousand dollars per concert at this time] to sing songs which essentially said they were shits. I figured it was probably cheaper than listening to a psychiatrist."

On November 12, 1967, they had received an impressive letter from Harry J. Kraut of the Boston Symphony Orchestra asking them to perform in the Shed at Tanglewood for the young musicians studying at the Berkshire Music Center. "It was like asking Mickey Mouse to lecture at Harvard," she said. "Our interest in having the Airplane," Kraut explained, ". . . stems from our increasing impression and awareness of the importance of pop music techniques and materials to the youngest generation of serious composers." They came recommended by Gunther Schuller, the influential dean of the New England Conservatory.

Grace's *tour de force* was performed on Thursday evening, October 3, 1968, at the Whitney Museum in New York. Airplane had been invited to play for the "friends of the Whitney," which Grace translated into big money. Wedged in between classical pianist Raymond Lewenthal and the light show of Glenn McKay, they were presented as a band of "sophisticated taste and highly refined technique who combined the echoes of In-

dian, Indonesian and Middle Eastern music as well as reflections
of Stravinsky in their repertoire." But as Grace wisely pointed
out: "They were coming to see a bunch of hippies put on a freak
show and I wasn't going to disappoint them."

She showed up at the Whitney that evening with a bottle of
Southern Comfort in her hand. "I wanted to get shit-faced for
this one. It was the perfect setup: a whole bunch of wealthy
snobs giving money to support the arts. It was Ripley's Believe It
or Not. I knew who these people were because I had once been
one of them, but we had gone in opposite directions. They
weren't there to listen to the music: they couldn't give a shit
about the Jefferson Airplane. They were only there because it
looked good on their income tax forms. And I wanted them to
know that we knew what they were up to."

It was the first time she got to use a wireless mike "so I was
free to walk around and talk to everyone on the elevators, in the
ladies' room and in their seats. As she stepped on stage, Paul shot
Spencer a look. "We knew what was coming," he smiled, "because we had seen her do this number before."

In front of the cognoscenti she rolled out a monologue which
addressed itself to "all you filthy jewels out there." Since her pro-
nunciation was slurred, the word "jewels" was misinterpreted as
"jews." "I didn't say anything they hadn't heard before," Grace
remarked. "I just told them it was good to be back in New York
with the rocks and Gucci loafers. I asked the women how it felt
to be sitting there in their tight girdles and not talking to their
husbands whom they only see at these functions, but never at
home in the bedroom."

The more the audience squirmed and cleared their throats, the
harder she came on. "I was just getting more and more intimi-
dating but I knew they were not going to say anything to me although every single person out there was thinking, fuck you."

In itself the opening monologue was merely a prelude to the
lyrics of their songs, which, if anybody could have understood
them, continued to put the audience down; but what people will
long remember was not the performance in itself but the fact
that during a short press conference Grace attacked the curator's

wife by asking her if she were sleeping with her husband or just living on his prestige. The curator demanded an apology but Grace was too drunk to even know what she was saying let alone recollect it for a coherent replay and apology. Amid the outrage and disgust of the patrons, Airplane simply faded into the dust on the following morning by flying out to San Francisco immediately.

Eight days later, a letter arrived from Stephen E. Weil, administrator of the Whitney Museum. "Will you tell each of the group for us how very appreciative we are of what they did to make . . . [the] evening such a success . . . I think we really did something that will be long remembered at the Museum. I'm afraid that Grace's opening monologue will also be long remembered."

13

With the release of *Crown of Creation* that summer, the band hit its stride. Though the New York *Times* and the Los Angeles *Times* wrote the album off as "mere poses, vainglorious exaggerations of what the group once was," the serious music publications like *Stereo Review* and *High Fidelity* were not as flip in their judgments. As Don Heckman wrote: "An earlier Airplane recording—*After Bathing at Baxter's*—was criticized for its abstractness, and the suggestion was made that the group had been reading too many of its press notices. I didn't agree. It seemed to me that the recording represented the kind of work that all artists must sometimes do—experimentation for its own sake, seeking rather than fulfilling. The seeds of many of these ideas have come to fruition in *Crown of Creation*." That record, in many ways, was Grace's finest hour as a stylist.

Grace was now proving to have an intuitive knack for relevant lyrics. Her "White Rabbit" was already the classic acid trip, and her "rejoyce" had opened the stream of consciousness of free love in popular music. "Lather" was the key song on the new album, and it projected an I'm-going-to-stay-young-if-it-kills-me image of her generation. Originally conceived as an impressionistic portrait of Spencer, the image broadened into the enlivenment of her popular concept of the "under thirty" generation. Like the imagery in her other songs, everybody agreed that it was brilliant, but, in all honesty, the RCA executives had no idea what to do with it.

For years the executives had selected their hits by following trends. Grace was obstinately original and too big a risk despite

her extraordinary hit in "White Rabbit." As a result of their deci-
sions, her songs were bypassed as singles for those of Paul
Kantner. By the time *Crown of Creation* was released, it was obvious that they basically wanted to use Grace as a figurehead for
publicity. As the fact became more and more evident, Grace told
herself and others that the neglect did not bother her. She herself bought and repeated the logic of the company as her own. "I
don't write hit singles," she remarked. Her actions belied her
words, however. When Spencer realized that RCA was not going
to develop Grace's potential as a songwriter, he convinced her to
fly down to Los Angeles with him to seek a contract with another company for a solo career. Grace was intrigued enough by
the possibilities to go through the motions with David Anderle of
Elektra, but in the final analysis she decided against it.

Whether or not she was serious about a solo career or just
playing games is a moot question; "I went to this party in
Beverly Hills with a lot of big recording executives from Los Angeles, like Herb Alpert, but it didn't work out. They seemed to
hide behind a shield of money, wall-to-wall sauna owners
discussing the acquisition of their new Spanish bath tiles and
wives, often in the same sentence." In the end, she flew back to
San Francisco to the band whom she was coming to regard as
"family." "Even if I earned less money there at least I was surrounded by my friends. Being a star in Los Angeles would get
very lonely."

The release of *Crown of Creation* had erased the blot on Airplane's reputation of *After Bathing at Baxter's* and had risen to
number 6 on the *Billboard* charts. More importantly, the album
marked the long-awaited maturation of the group's music. "For
the first time," said Grace, "we were all aiming at pretty much
the same concept in our songs. It wasn't that we sat around and
planned our lyrics together. Each of us usually worked separately (and unrelatedly) on our songs, but I think the relative
failure of *Baxter's* scared us into a hit."

Though the recording sessions in Los Angeles remained as
chaotic as ever, the band did not take their experimentations as

seriously. "If it worked, we put it on the album. If not, we left it on the floor of the control room. I guess after *Baxter's* we realized that we couldn't afford the risks."

The album was produced with a coherence and unified sensibility which even *Surrealistic Pillow* lacked, with all its sensitivity and delicacy of style. Some critics, notably *Rolling Stone,* felt that Airplane had surrendered their spontaneity, but as Grace saw it, "we were just starting to grow up in the studio. When we first began, none of us knew what we were doing. We were exploring electronic sounds and hoping to create new dimensions in electric music. What we wanted to do, maybe unconsciously at the time, was share our enthusiasm. We wanted the public to hear our exploration because we felt that the experiments were as exciting as the end results. What we learned is that nobody really wanted to sit around and listen to all the songs which didn't quite work out. Most people don't want to hear all of Leonard Bernstein's wrong notes."

So the group had set about cleaning up their act on February 20 in Los Angeles when they began recording the album. Grace was the first one with complete material, during the early weeks of March. She had written both her songs for this album eight months earlier when the band had been living in a luxurious five-thousand-dollar-a-month mansion in Beverly Hills. It is no accident that both "Greasy Heart" and "Lather" contain similar metaphors, though they deal with different subjects. The lyrics are concerned with the toys and playthings of adults. "We were really children," Grace remarked of the band, "and trying hard to stay that way." That realization was expressed in these songs. " 'Greasy Heart' was my own version of Marty Balin's 'Plastic Fantastic Lover.' His lyrics are observations about how people often replace a lover with a television set." Grace's treatment of the same theme is intensely personal in its language and development. "What I am essentially telling plastic people is not to take acid. It would blow their whole charade and they would be left in a marathon run without crutches."

The song on the album which most revealed the versatility of her styling was "Triad." It was written by David Crosby, who first played it for her over at the RCA studios during the recording of *Baxter's*. "He was writing about his experience, not mine," Grace clarified. "I never balled two guys in one bed." The texture of the song interested her because "I have a definite sympathy with that situation, although I never could pull off a ménage à trois myself. I have enough trouble with one-to-one relationships."

The rest of the album is a sensitive expression of the new perspective which crystallized in the phrase "Life is change" in the title song "Crown of Creation" by Paul Kantner. The unity of the tracks is derived from the coherence of this perspective. To achieve it, the band canned a lot of material. Except for "Chushingura," a one-minute-and-seventeen-second instrumental, all of Spencer's songs were thrown out, including "The Saga of Sidney Spacepig," "Ribumbabap Rubadubadumdum" and other momentary impulses. "His sensibility was different from the rest of the band," Grace said. "They were willing to try anything once. But after the failure of *Baxter's,* they weren't going to record anything too off-the-wall."

Also falling into this category, unfortunately, was a collaboration inspired by Spencer between Grace and Frank Zappa. "It was a lot less exciting than you might think," Spencer admitted. "It was just a wild electronic improvisation." It was entitled "Would You Like a Snack," and was instantly thrown in the can.

The recording of *Crown of Creation* marked the diminishing influence of Spencer on Grace. Still the best drummer around, his antics and sense of humor antagonized the other musicians. Through these sessions Grace found herself in greater harmony with Paul Kantner. "But Paul had quite a few women around," she said, "and I wasn't thinking about becoming one of them."

Some time earlier during the band's tour of Europe, the two experienced the mutual recognition of a strong attraction. While the band was doing acid on a boat trip, Kantner became quietly confused. He had been sitting on the boat while everyone else was running around on a little island they had found. Grace noticed that Paul wasn't joining in the fun, and went over to see if there was anything she could do to make him feel better. She put her arms around him and reminded him that it was just the acid, and that the confusion would disappear when the chemical wore off. Up to this fateful moment, their relationship, according to Kantner, was like an "Emily Brontë situation, a passing glance, a brush on the shoulder." Now as she put her arms around him—merely a gesture of comfort—he felt attraction. "I had a weird feeling in my stomach," said Grace, "but I thought it was sympathetic confusion."

A few weeks later, on September 14, the band flew out of Amsterdam with a week off. Spencer and Grace took off for a week in St. Thomas. Paul joined them there after four days, at a posh motel called the Lime Tree. He was with one of his occasional girls. "I remember going up to his room to bum a cigarette," Grace said. "It was ridiculous. There was a cigarette machine right outside my room and I don't even smoke his brand."

When she saw the other girl, "I felt a vague pang of jealousy." The next day Grace left, leaving Spencer behind. "She told me she had discovered this cockroach in our bed and that she had to get out of there because the bugs were driving her batty."

By November 28, when the band returned to New York to play the Fillmore East, their romance was all but finished, though Grace couldn't admit to herself that it was ending. "I knew I didn't want to live with the guy," she said, "but I figured in some way I was still in love with him." A certain degree of unacknowledged resentment had, however, grown up between them. Spencer was too emotional for her. She was too autonomous for him. On the last night of their New York performance, when Spencer was drunk, he picked up a groupie out of the audience. Flaunting her, he drove back to the Gramercy Park Hotel in the limousine with Grace on one side and the girl on the other. The triad walked into the lobby, then into the elevator. "When I got to my room," he said, "I just smiled at Grace, ushered the girl in and closed my door."

Grace flew back to San Francisco with the band on the following morning of December 1. "I didn't feel any anger or pain," she says. "There were always girls around the band." Spencer remained behind wallowing in guilt and alcohol. A few days later, he flew back to San Francisco to find that the apartment, which he had left in the hands of two groupies during the tour, had burned down.

14

Grace was down in Los Angeles at the recording studio mastering tapes for the group's first live album, entitled *Bless Its Pointed Little Head*. The actual taping had taken place at the Fillmore West October 25, 26 and 27 of 1968. Now she and Paul Kantner were the last members of the band left in the control room, pinpointing unnoticed errors and correcting certain sounds. "Even before this album, Paul and I were usually the last ones to leave the studio because we were the ones concerned with the mechanical details."

On this particular occasion, December 13, "we were sitting at the control board, on which there were hundreds of knobs. He was running something and I was running something else which was right next to him. Our hands accidentally brushed each other, and nobody said a thing, but the gesture had definitely become a remark. A very definite remark."

While all this was happening, Spencer was getting ready to move into the big house. "I was in limbo," he explained, and Jorma and Margaretta, whose apartment was also demolished in the fire "had decided to move in there as an interim kind of thing."

The "big house" was a recent acquisition of the band. Bill Thompson had originally suggested investing their money in real estate as offices, and, Spencer admitted, "we did because it was the only thing we could all agree on."

With the aid of his secretary Jacky Watts, who eventually married Jorma's brother Peter, Thompson started combing the city and finally ended up purchasing a renowned white elephant at a "real estate bargain basement sale." The three-floor structure, now in need of paint and furnishing, had once enjoyed a certain degree of elegance. Built in 1904 or so and later used as a shelter during the San Francisco earthquake and fire by Enrico Caruso, it already had a distinguished heritage when Thompson bought it for sixty-five thousand dollars from a ninety-three-year-old rancher who apparently did not believe in upkeep.

The musicians had not planned on living there as a commune in the beginning; but several weeks after the purchase, Paul lay claim to the biggest room on the top floor and moved in with his own housekeeper, Barbara, who earned room and board by attending to his basic needs. Though Thompson wanted to charge rent, "Paul argued him out of it," said Spencer, "and convinced Thompson to pick up the utility bill, too. We were all supposed to chip in for food and things but there were so many people around freeloading it didn't work out, and Paul hit Thompson for seventy-five dollars a week." There was an arsenal of drugs: tanks of nitrous oxide, cocaine, fine acid and high-quality marijuana which Paul stashed in elegant decanters throughout his room. "They were the nouveau riche of Haight-Ashbury," remarked Jerry Slick. "They had made it."

When Grace flew back to San Francisco from Los Angeles, she heard about the fire and headed over to the big house to find Spencer. Instead of Spencer, however, she ran into Sally Mann, an old girl friend of Paul's. "I talked to Sally for a long time. I really liked her because she was intelligent and had a perverse sense of humor. She was good-looking and I appreciate good looks, especially when they come with a brain."

Sally was kind of curious about when the rest of the band was coming back to the big house and, Grace said, "by the time we finished talking I knew that it was over between me and Spencer. Sally never even mentioned his name but I knew that she was there for Spencer and I would eventually be with Paul."

At the moment, however, the fires were only starting to burn between Sally and Spencer. The two had only become reacquainted during the week Grace was away. "While I was packing up the remains of the apartment," Spencer recalled, "Jorma called me upstairs in the burned-out wreck to meet this chick Sally Mann. She was with one of Paul's other girl friends, Karen, and they were both real nice-looking so I thought I'd make a date. I asked them to come over to the big house, acted real charming, took Sally into Marty's room and spent the night with her. She started just coming around with a lot of coke and we started an affair. Grace was still down in L.A. having an affair with Graham Nash," a liaison she frankly denies, "though I wouldn't have minded it at the time," she adds.

By Grace's return to San Francisco on December 14, the coals were already in the fire. Spencer began spending more and more time with Sally while still maintaining his close relationship with Grace. Grace invited Jerry Slick to move in with her in Sausalito. "It was not a reconciliation," she said; "it was just the right arrangement at that time." Though living with Jerry, she continued seeing Spencer. They went out driving one morning and talked about how goofy the whole thing was. But when she left, she still didn't know any more about how to smooth it out than she had before they started. Spencer sensed this, and wrote her a long letter describing his feelings a few days later. "It was filled with hurt and confusion but it was very beautiful because it was so honest." What he essentially said was that he loved her, "but I don't know what to do about it." Then without apologies, he admitted that "Sally was in my life. It may or may not be right but that's the way it is. I know it's the shits. I'm sorry. I love both of you." Grace thought, "Okay, I can't change him, so I'll change me, or Smirnoff will change me." That night she polished off what there was in the way of vodka in the liquor cabinet.

Spencer, who had salvaged barely half his stuff, bought new things for his room on the second floor. "I made up a little room for Grace," he said, "which turned out to be a *big* mistake."

One night Grace surprised him around midnight by deciding to stay over. She knocked on his door and found Sally with him listening to records. Spencer turned green, then tried to make the cohabitation look reasonable by reintroducing Sally as the new live-in downstairs cook and housekeeper.

The plot thickened a few days later when two groupies from the Fillmore East showed up on the doorstep looking for Spencer. "I was in bed with one of them," he said, "when Sally walked in. She went downstairs to tell Grace what a shit I was for two-timing both of them. So there I was apologizing to Grace for Sally and trying to tell Sally it would never work between us. I guess I fucked up one too many times, though, and nobody was listening to me. All of a sudden I saw Grace offering Sally a slug of Southern Comfort, and the two of them started walking around drinking together like best buddies, commiserating about what a shit I was."

The drinking went on that night while Spencer was hopelessly trying to cool all his women down. The groupies left, Grace and Sally got drunker and drunker. "I can remember at one point," noted Spencer, "that Grace and I were sitting together on the stairs crying and asking each other why this had to happen to us."

Finally, around 5 A.M., Grace stopped crying and began getting angry. "We got her up to Paul's room, where she was bemoaning the whole weird situation and carrying on with loud, unstoppable dialogue. She kept asking for Paul," Spencer said. Spencer called Jerry Slick for help. "I told him that I just couldn't handle her this way." Jerry drove into the city, picked up Grace and stayed with her for the next few days in Sausalito.

Bless Its Pointed Little Head was released in February, and at the very time Grace was experiencing this depressing change of partners, *Newsweek* was singling Joplin and her out as the first females strong enough to liberate the woman in rock and roll. "In a group," she told the reporter, "you have to get used to functioning as a guy does. It definitely makes you more masculine—either that or you go crazy."

By the early months of 1969, three months after the student strike at San Francisco State, Grace had gotten herself back together. She had become tight friends with Sally, who was now going with Spencer. Grace's career was at its height. With the conscience of the nation astir over the Vietnam War, the student protests and the proven corruption of the high-standing members of the establishment (on May 15 Supreme Court justice Abe Fortas resigned after *Life* magazine revealed that he had accepted a twenty-thousand-dollar bribe), Grace's outspoken rhetoric and her endorsements of acid were taking on increasing importance. Her status in the counterculture attracted the powers in Hollywood; in fact, Otto Preminger, who was attending the radical chic parties of Leonard Bernstein and dropping acid behind the sets, made the journey down to the recording studio in Los Angeles to offer her a role. "It was less a meeting than a confrontation," Bill Thompson reported. "Preminger sat around trying to convince Grace that he was just another hippie." Grace listened smugly, then nailed him, face to face, as a hypocrite. "I couldn't see many redeeming social factors in his movie [entitled *Skidoo*] about Jackie Gleason dropping acid." The next script submitted to her was for the film *Big Fauss and Little Halsey.* "I read it and thought it stank so I turned it down. I still didn't want to do anything about Mary kissing John—that's repetitious unless the scriptwriter's a genius. People were getting killed, so who cares if John gets Mary in the middle of it?" Robert Redford and Michael J. Pollard starred in the film, with Lauren Hutton playing the part that Grace had rejected.

The Airplane did touch base, however, with a more avant-garde filmmaker, Jean-Luc Godard. "We met him in some office," said Grace, "and he could have been an insurance salesman. He was trying to impress us as a nifty filmmaker and we were trying to impress him as cool and bizarre musicians. It was an hour of pleasant bullshit."

The project interested them enough for them to agree to co-star in it and compose special music. A delighted Godard announced to the press: "The Jefferson Airplane is the only rock group in the world that is me." Like the Airplane and their music, Godard improvised the scripts of his films. "So we were only told to go to 57 West Forty-fifth Street at twelve-thirty on a Friday afternoon and set up our equipment to play on the roof of the Schuyler Hotel," remembered Bill Thompson. "Across the street, from a window on the tenth-floor offices of the Leacock-Pennebaker studios, Godard was shooting us."

The scene was set on the ninth floor of the hotel, where actor Rip Torn, who was wearing a red scarf around his neck, and Paula Matter, wrapped in a bedsheet, were perched dangerously on the windowsill waking up to the sound of the Airplane. "But nobody told us they were there," remarked Thompson. "We just set up our amplifiers and started to play 'Somebody to Love,' then 'We Can Be Together.'" In a rock club the sound would have been loud, but in midtown Manhattan with bumper-to-bumper traffic, "it was astounding." Grace said: "You could hear the brakes screeching and see the pedestrians frozen in their tracks." Marty yelled out an amplified: "Wake up, New York. Wake up!"

In the middle of the second song, a policeman appeared and ordered the Airplane to stop. "But we figured it would make a better film if we were irritating," Grace said. She continued singing with the rest of the band. Moments later, there were *five* cops, and Rip Torn and Paula Matter made *their* entrance only to be hassled by the cops pushing them. When they resisted, they were both put under arrest and taken in a squad car to the 18th Precinct—as the Airplane continued playing. "We figured we should at least finish the set," quipped Grace.

On December 17, 1969, the film, entitled *One American Movie,* opened at the Telegraph Avenue Repertory Cinema in Berkeley. "It is a fascinating sequence and the film itself, actually only a work print of a series of interviews plus some footage of Rip Torn which hints at what the flick might have ultimately been, does something which I find quite important," wrote Ralph Gleason. "In a way, it is an exact mirror of the political scene today . . . It is a collection of open-end raps which ultimately becomes boring . . . If it were not for the presence of the rock band and the fact that its footage is not only interesting visually but also listenable, the whole thing would have been hard to take."

Grace had her second node operation in January. It went smoothly, but she couldn't talk for a month. Instead, she jotted notes, drew sketches and did the things people do that don't require speech. Upon her recovery, the Airplane flew to Honolulu to play at the International Centre on March 8. While there they rented a Spanish castle on the ocean for a week. "It was the most romantic scenery I had ever seen," Grace said;

"tropical flowers, Polynesian groupies, piña coladas around the pool and long walks on the beaches." Grace was with Spencer again in Hawaii, "but I had more or less had it with him. There we were in this beautiful romantic setting and he was taking uppers and coming down with alcohol and sleeping all day long. I finally couldn't stand hanging around in a room with the shades drawn all day." With feelings of guilt and disloyalty, she wandered out to the pool to see if anyone wanted to go into town. Paul was there and offered her some orange sunshine. "It was real good stuff, early acid, and we just snipped off a little piece of the tablet."

Though the rain clouds were gathering, they hooked up with Jorma and Margaretta and went driving around the hills. "It was the first time Paul and I were alone doing something which had nothing to do with the studio or records or the band. It was a pleasure to get to know him on a freer basis."

As the rain came pouring down, the acid began to take effect. "It wasn't particularly tender because I was still supposed to be with Spencer and Paul had a girl friend at the house. But I was conscious for the first time of his gentleness. Usually he was the iron will type, but that day it was a pleasure to see some of his softness come through." Kantner was having the same response to her and a few weeks later after rehearsal in San Francisco, they went back to the big house together. "I made him a real WASP dinner of meat and potatoes," she said, "and he invited me up to his bedroom for a bottle of champagne."

The next morning, Bill Thompson spotted them coming downstairs together. "She had a sheepish grin on her face and he looked pretty satisfied. And I thought, 'Oh no, here we go again.'"

15

Assistant Attorney General Richard Kleindienst called a national press conference in May of 1969 to warn the nation about the existence of "ideological criminals" roaming freely in the streets. "When you see an epidemic like this cropping up all over the country—the same kind of people saying the same kinds of things—you begin to get the picture that it is a national subversive activity."

That summer thousands upon thousands of ideological criminals made the pilgrimage to the Airplane's free concerts across the country—at Grant Park in Chicago on May 13, the Carousal in San Francisco on July 7, Griffith Park in Los Angeles on July 28, and on August 10, the Sheep Meadow in Central Park in Manhattan, where the crowd numbered over fifty thousand. "We thought the main interest in New York was the legitimate theater, so having fifty thousand New Yorkers wanting to listen to us was both an honor and something of a joke. But they were warm and open, and very patient about being sardined in a crowd of that size."

The next job was the Tanglewood Music Festival. With an audience of more than six thousand people in the Shed where the Boston Symphony Orchestra normally performed, they played with B. B. King and the Who in Tanglewood's first rock concert. From Massachusetts they went to Liberty, New York, and Woodstock.

The band had learned about Woodstock months earlier in New York from Chip Monck, a young and highly competent lighting man and production manager who was "all fired up about this idea of bringing a lot of bands together in one place out in the country." Grace recalled his initial description: "They would set up about fifty tents where people would be hand-carving, sewing and creating the things that represented our culture. They were going to rig up a massive stage, build thirty-foot towers for all the spotlights and construct a place where everybody could get first aid if they needed it. It was supposed to be a gathering of a new crowd of people who wanted to get together and listen to the new bands for three days. The prospect of this thing working was very interesting. I had a lot of hope that he and his friends could pull it off."

The only precedent for this kind of event was the Monterey Pop Festival two years earlier; its omens, unfortunately, had not been positive. Barely a month after Monterey, the spirit of brotherly love had been tinged by the possibility of financial exploitation. Attorneys were retained by the Monterey Pop Festival and the Airplane, Big Brother and the Holding Company and other rock bands. Bob Gordon of the law firm Baerwitz and Gordon inquired about the monies from television syndication. Allan Biblin of Mitchell, Silberberg and Knupp, representing the promotors, deflected his inquiry by assuring the bands that any profits would be used "for charitable purposes." The inquiry into money, he went on, "is hardly in keeping with the spirit of the festival." In short, no money was distributed to the bands. And any donation to charities went unrecorded in the accounting books of the bands.

Bill Thompson learned the lesson and negotiated fiercely for top dollar for the band to perform at Woodstock. "Jimi Hendrix got the most," Thompson said. "He got seventeen thousand five hundred dollars and we got second high over everybody else, fifteen thousand dollars." To the musicians, however, who were now receiving around two hundred and fifty dollars a week with an occasional five-thousand-dollar bonus and publishing royalties, "what we made at Woodstock was relatively unimportant," said Grace. "I wasn't thinking about performing there only for the money. I was fascinated by the prospect of having that many people living together for several days with almost constant music."

The Airplane was among the first bands to check in at the

Holiday Inn. Bill Thompson, who got room #1, was struck by the symbolism of the name Liberty for the town. "Dale Franklin, who was Bill Graham's secretary at the Fillmore East, had been up there for a week," Spencer recalled. "The rumor was that she didn't eat or sleep. She just hung out in the lobby with her clipboard, directing traffic." She asked them what band they were and assigned them rooms. As the best-laid plans go astray, however, a shortage of accommodations began to develop as soon as they checked in. "At one point," Bill Thompson said, "Joan Baez, Sly Stone, Ravi Shankar, the Grateful Dead and Janis Joplin were all in the lobby waiting to find out if they could get a room." Some transferred over to the Howard Johnson's because the Holiday Inn, according to Spencer, was getting "maniacal, like Grand Central Station. There were times when it felt like the whole rock world was standing at the desk asking for their keys."

Sally had checked in with Spencer. Grace, who was now occasionally with Paul, took her own room. "If I had been with Richard Nixon, I wouldn't have noticed him at Woodstock. It was massive chaos. Nobody actually knew what was happening but that kind of joyous confusion brought us together. I was with everybody."

On the first day, Grace went for a swim in the pool at the Holiday Inn—but that was the extent of her socializing. "She pretty much kept to herself," said Bill's secretary Jacky Watts; "she's sociable but just not social." Though she occasionally dropped into the bar, she did not hang out with Jacky or Spencer, who were playing poker with Keith Moon and Janis Joplin. "It was pouring rain outside and we could hear the rhythm of the drops in the bar, which was filled with wall-to-wall musicians from San Francisco. Everybody was high on something. We all took tons of acid or got dosed. I drank a glass of vodka—and found out later it had seventy-five hundred mikes of acid in it," said Jacky. "I was totally out of commission for the entire next day."

While the other musicians were partying, Grace went over to check out the site. It was originally situated in Wallkill, New York, but when the Wallkill Concerned Citizens Committee protested against the event, the promoters transferred it to the six-hundred-acre dairy farm of Max Yasgur, a forty-nine-year-old hippie who received a fifty-thousand dollar check for the rental. The weather was inclement from the start and rain seemed likely.

In the early afternoon Grace and Paul roamed the premises together. "It was the day before anybody got there and all these guys were running around with hard hats on. They were trying to put together this big stage, setting up lights, scaffolding—the whole routine. I was fascinated by the whole setup—not frightened but excited by the acres and acres of barren fields which I knew would soon be filled with hundreds and thousands of people like us. That was the interesting thing about Woodstock. Everybody was equal. The common denominator was music, youth and marijuana. There wasn't going to be much coke or harder stuff, and I think that was one reason for the good vibes."

"Everybody looked whacked out because they were so fucking stoned," added Jacky Watts, "but Grace was the touch of class in the field. She looked immaculate that Saturday when she came out of her room to go over to the stage. She hadn't done any drugs for days before the performance. She was radiant."

Meanwhile, back at the hotel, Bill Thompson was running around organizing. He had learned a critical lesson from the unfortunate aftermath of the Monterey Pop Festival. With the managers of the Who, the Grateful Dead, Creedence Clearwater and Santana, he stepped forward and demanded that the bands be paid *before* they performed. The promoters were resistant and "kept telling me it was all peace and love," Thompson said. "They said everything was groovy. I finally told them that I'd only feel brotherly love for them after they handed over the check." Though it was Saturday and the banks were closed, they obviously could not afford to risk losing these bands. "They bitched all the way to the bank," smiled Thompson, "but they managed to get someone to open the vault and they turned over the certified checks to me." (It was a masterful stroke. Later more than six hundred thousand dollars in bad checks bounced.)

The Airplane came in along the back road through the long

stream of mud puddles toward the stage. "The wind was blowing hard. It was raining. Owsley, who had an eye on Grace, was giving away acid to the bands. Around two we all dropped acid and it started coming on real fast. There was this big screen hanging over our heads and it was billowing in the wind. For a moment, I thought I was flying on the side of the stage," Spencer said, "then I realized that was ridiculous. It felt more like a sailing ship."

The platform was in the middle of several thousand people, so the musicians had a lot of trouble going anywhere other than the stage.

"We didn't have much choice," said Paul; "either we could sit on the stage (there were no chairs) or down in the mud puddles. They had some great fruit lying around for us to eat and I can remember listening to the music munching these grapes. We kept getting ready to go on. There really was tremendous momentum in the beginning, but then we'd hear that Sly was late and Janis had to play at a specific time. Airplane kept getting bumped."

"What bothered me," added Grace, "was that there weren't any facilities around. I sat there for more than ten hours without going to the bathroom."

Creedence Clearwater played. Janis played. Sly played. The Who played. Abbie Hoffman grabbed the microphone because he wanted to say something. But Pete Townshend didn't like him interrupting the Who's set so he hit him over the head with his guitar. (Later Hoffman apologized to him for freaking out.) Grace listened and watched through her sunglasses with eyes half shut. "I was tired, so tired that I didn't know if we were going to make it or not but we figured what the hell. If we came this far we might as well slide right on through."

Before her was "a massive audience. There was no end to the people. A lot of them were asleep because, like us, they'd been up all night. A lot of them were cheering, others were zonked out. What I noticed was that everybody looked happy. There must have been five hundred thousand people around us. We were unable to move because there were even a hundred thousand people in back of us. Even though we were tired, wet and crowded, we all felt like it was more than worth whatever inconveniences occurred." The Airplane performed, according to Thompson, between six-thirty and eight-thirty in the morning. "That was nine hours later than we were supposed to go on," noted Grace. As she moved to the front of the stage, she could see the sun rising over the sleepy faces of the people who had come to hear the music that represented freedom for their generation.

16

Paul bought the first waterbed for the big house. Despite some inconveniences, it served a purpose. "Nobody made a big deal about it," Grace explained, "but if you happened to run into somebody and you didn't have anything else to do, you could either go down to the kitchen for a cup of tea or up to the waterbed for a quickie." Grace was amused by the ironic fact that the top floor had probably once been run as a brothel around half a century ago. Now it served as an arena of free love. "Not everybody was into it; there are degrees of free love. We were all different people. There was no pressure to ball a guy or not to ball him; everybody just did what they wanted to do. I've heard other bands say that they were having a zoo come in tonight, which means three or four women at once and leaving them the next night, but Airplane was very respectful of women. There was one girl, Detroit Frieda, who gave one of the guys the clap, then she came back a month later and he balled her again. He got the clap again. What did he expect? It became a running joke in the band."

By the fall of 1969, flower children across the country were making pilgrimages to the big house, which had become the most infamous commune in the country. The Airplane usually served marijuana to their guests. "Paul was always asking Thompson for money to buy stuff," said Spencer. The friends of the Airplane got to partake in the riches. "People were always hanging out there."

Janis Joplin, who was a tight friend of Marty, would occasionally drop by to shoot pool, although she and Grace were not particularly close. David Crosby would hang out and play songs

Above, Spencer Dryden.
Photo courtesy of Spencer Dryden.

Left, sunrise at Woodstock.
Photo courtesy of RCA.

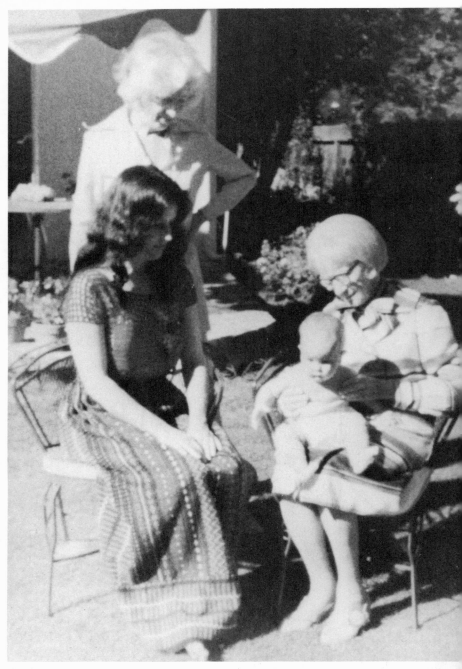

Four generations. From left: Virginia Wing, Grace Slick, China Kantner and Lady Sue. *Photo courtesy of Virginia Wing.*

Above,
the nuclear family:
China, Paul and Grace.
Photo courtesy of Virginia Wing.

Left, China Kantner.
Photo courtesy of Grace Johnson.

Mr. and Mrs. Skip Johnson. *Photo courtesy of Grace Johnson.*

efferson Starship. From left: Aynsley Dunbar, David Freiberg, Mickey Thomas, Craig Chaquico, Pete Sears, Paul Kantner. © *1979 by Roger Ressmeyer.*

A typical rock star of the 1970s. *Photo by Ron Galella.*

Skip and Grace at home. *Photo by Ron Galella.*

Grace Johnson, 1979. *Photo by Skip Johnson.*

for the band which, like "Wooden Ships," would from time to time appear on their albums. "The lyrics of that song never completely made sense," noted David Freiberg—it was a collaboration between Crosby, Kantner and Steve Stills—"but that's because Kantner said they were stoned when they came up with it."

One morning Spencer met Al Kooper walking down the hill from Stanyan Avenue. "He had on these colorful patched pants, snakeskin boots and big shades. I asked him to drop by for some coffee," Spencer recalled. "He stayed for seven to ten days. I didn't ever figure out why."

Rip Torn, who had been arrested during the filming in New York of the Godard film, and his wife Geraldine Page struck up a long-term friendship with the band. "They wanted us to do *Richard III*," said Grace, "as a satire against the Nixon regime, and I thought it was a pretty good idea." Their conception was to perform outdoors in the round with the full band performing an original score, a troupe of actors and real battle scenes with audience participation. But we would have had to tour for a year, and the complicated logistics were staggering, and additionally, some of the band members didn't like the idea of performing the same specific works over and over again." Torn did eventually go on to do *Richard* in New York, performing the role as Richard Nixon.

Though every musician in the band owned equal shares of the big house along with Bill Thompson, Paul was turning out to be more equal than anybody else. With the largest room, an arsenal of dope stashed in elegant decanters around the room and an entourage of female friends, he was the master of the big house, though everybody was loath to admit it. Shy to the point of retirement and rigid in comportment, Kantner had a strength of purpose which made him more decisive than any of the other musicians and earned him the nickname of the Nazi. He had grown up in St. Joseph's Military Academy after his mother died. "I was four or six or something like that," he said, "and I don't remember very much about her except whenever I didn't do what she wanted me to do, she threatened to throw me in the oven."

His parents were divorced before her death and his father was a salesman away a lot on the road. Kantner was consequently raised by the Jesuits in a Catholic military school, a highly formal and unemotional environment.

"Paul Kantner is a composite of a bunch of stuff," said Grace. "For the most part he's largely misunderstood. I think 98 per cent of the people who know him well consider him cold, not self-centered but rigid, but he is also very kind, generous and adaptable to chaotic situations—and I'm walking chaos."

Though Grace was still living with Jerry, she would stay over at the big house with Paul two or three times a week. "I liked having a lot of girl friends," Paul explained, "but most want to be the only one. I had only lived once with one girl for any length of time before this. Most girls just don't give me enough time to myself."

Grace did not pose this kind of problem, however; in fact, her excessive autonomy which had irked Spencer and even Jerry worked to her advantage with Kantner. Through the fall of 1969, they carried on a casual affair. "When I'd go over to talk to Paul," said David Freiberg, then with Quicksilver Messenger Service, "she would just *be* there. He wouldn't explain and I remember thinking that as a couple they were strange."

It was a loose arrangement. In addition to Jerry in Sausalito she was hanging out with Spencer and Sally, who had become her closest friends. "Occasionally I would become friends with one of Paul's other girl friends, too. Other people might have found that unusual, but it seemed natural to me because we had so much in common. The strongest bond between two women might be their mutual love of one man."

Though Woodstock had proven a strong confirmation of her values, her own life was becoming increasingly complicated. On July 6, after a benefit at the Fillmore West, she was attacked on the streets of San Francisco by two men. "They were carrying some hot metal thing, and they hit me in the mouth with it." One of them grabbed her and reached for her purse. No shrinking vi-

7

olet, Grace pretended to faint. As her body went limp she slithered out of their grasp and ran for her life, her purse in hand. "I was not scared," she told the musicians at the big house afterward.

On November 26 at the Fillmore East, she added another anecdote to her legacy by walking into the spotlight dressed as Adolf Hitler. With her hair slicked back and completely outfitted in mustache and uniform, she bore a striking resemblance to the German dictator. Later Rip Torn turned up on stage dressed as Richard Nixon. "I figured it was the right double play," she said. "The two definitely had a lot in common."

By the fall tour of 1969, the band was working overtime. To keep the pace, most of them were doing speed. "We played hundreds of gigs between early 1968 and 1970," said Bill Laudner, former Prankster who was now the Airplane's road manager. "We were really working hard, and around September of 1969 Grace started experiencing a lot of weird things, but she never complained."

In November after a gig at Penn State University, the band flew back to the hotel in New York City and checked in around 2:30 A.M. Paul and Grace had adjoining rooms but Paul couldn't open his door because there was a chain on the other side. Grace walked into her room, turned on the lights and quietly announced that there was a man on her bed. "So I roared into her room," Laudner went on, "and grabbed the guy off the bed and dragged him out into the hall threatening him. He remained real passive, didn't fight back. He was very calm. He just kept insisting that he was Grace's husband and the father of her child.

"Grace wasn't hysterical. She was standing there calmly saying that she had never seen the guy before in her life. No one was real upset," said Laudner, "except me because the guy wouldn't do anything. He didn't care about my threats. They didn't faze him. He just stuck to his story. He wouldn't leave."

Eventually they called the police. When they arrived, the mystery man just repeated that Grace was his wife and the mother of their child. "Everything he was saying appeared to make sense," admitted Laudner, "and we had difficulty convincing the police that he was crazy. After a while, he even started to make sense to us."

The police eventually dragged him off but there were other guys who climbed in her twentieth-floor hotel room to wait for her in bed after the show. And photo exhibitionists who sent her pictures of their penises for her reactions. One even began coming around the big house with a gun threatening to kill himself if she didn't ball him. "She never complained," said Laudner. "She experienced a lot of weird things but she never got hysterical or bitchy or anything like that. She just didn't want to be bothered by people. More than anything she started to withdraw."

The police started hassling the group during the fall of 1969 in every city across the country. "We'd play longer than we were supposed to," said Paul, "and the kids would be dancing in the aisles. The cops didn't like that. They'd turn the lights on and turn off the sound. A lot of times Spencer would just play drums and we'd lead the audience in a chant or the lyrics of one of our songs. It was happening so regularly that we were going to get our own battery-powered amplifier to turn on when they turned our power off; but then we figured we should just hire our own policeman to come out and turn us off at the end of our shows."

In Houston Paul blew a bullhorn and the cops cut the power off. Paul started yelling to the kids not to let the cops do it to them. "The cops surrounded him and told the band to get out of town," recalled Thompson. "Paul was very antagonistic in those days. In Miami when we were down at Pirate's World, they cut the power off when Paul said something to the kids like let's burn the place down. The cops busted him. I went over to bail him out immediately but he made so much of a scene that they moved him into a room where all these cops were sitting around drinking Bourbon. Paul shuffled their papers around and spiked their booze with acid. Nobody was looking."

In New Orleans, the cops kicked down the door in the room where Jack, Bill Laudner and Paul were hanging out. "It was miraculous," said Thompson, "because nobody had anything on them except this one girl who was with us. She had two joints. At that time they could have put us away for five years for that.

We got this famous lawyer Henry Rothblatt who did the Green Berets or something big like that." In Dallas, they got into a whole other number when the police began tape-recording concerts and fining rock stars five hundred dollars for every "bad" word mentioned during the gig. "With Grace's mouth," Paul said, "it could get real expensive. They were trying to bust Jim Morrison for his language and we knew about that. But in Texas the police chief sends these assholes down to the gig. He had his men surround us while he started telling us that we couldn't talk like that. I think Grace had said fuck or something."

The most dramatic confrontation took place in Honolulu on October 17 when Paul was busted for possession of marijuana. "It was a plant," said Bill Thompson. "The cops planted a joint on him. What made it embarrassing for him was that it was this thin little joint. Paul would rather be caught dead than smoke something that terrible."

The day before the cops moved in on him Paul had given an interview. "The reporter set me up and wrote about us smoking joints. This must have irritated some of the upper-crust ladies, who alerted the cops, who put our house under surveillance. As we pulled in from the gig, our road manager spotted the police all around us. I was sneaking around the seawall along the ocean to check them out when they grabbed me. They dragged me into the foyer, thrust me on the ground and handcuffed me behind my back and started questioning."

The other members of the band gathered around to watch the cops arresting him. "We were all just sitting around laughing at the cops and drinking while they kept on threatening us. They were trying to play it straight and none of us was taking them very seriously, which drove them crazy," recalled Spencer. "Finally they pulled out this miserable excuse for a roach and one guy said it had fallen out of Paul's pocket onto the sand."

"We were all just cracking up and getting another drink as they were arresting Paul, who kept mimicking them and imitating one of the guys' voices, with them arguing their brains out," said Grace. "I thought it was pretty funny because I knew we had enough money to get him out of the can, so it was no big deal getting arrested. It was nothing to get upset about. Either you could view it as amusing or annoying."

They took Paul down to jail, where "some dumb guy kept reading me my rights and asking me if I understood what he was saying. I kept telling him no. So they put me in a holding cell with this black guy who didn't have anybody to bail him out. So I had the band bail him out, too."

When the matter went to court, "they found me guilty of a misdemeanor, which meant I had to pay a fine. That's all. I stood up to the judge and told him that I thought the sentence was stupid. I said that I thought the main reason they were having so much trouble with youth these days was because the courts were such a sham. The judge turned purple and told me to sit down. The fine was around three hundred and fifty dollars."

Afterward at lunch with the attorney, Paul was persuaded to take the decision all the way to the Supreme Court. "The lawyer told me that we were now proceeding with the theory that marijuana was not a drug and consequently the arrests for its possession were an invasion of privacy. I thought the lawyer, Hyman Goldstein, was a real sincere guy. His aim was to help a lot of kids fucked up by the marijuana laws and I thought it was a good cause though I didn't expect to win. [It got thrown out of court before it reached the Supreme Court.] I just like to disturb the legal machinery now and then."

The next album, entitled *Volunteers,* was released in November of 1969. Its tracks were the first ones laid down by a rock band in a San Francisco recording studio. "The band didn't buy all the horseshit about the best studios being down in L.A.," said Grace. "When it got right down to it, they wanted to sleep in their own beds."

By April 27, 1969, when Wally Heider opened his recording studio down in the Tenderloin on Hyde Street, San Francisco was already mecca to the rock industry. Local musicians had released more than sixty albums; fifteen of the first nineteen were best sellers nationally. Jefferson Airplane, the Quicksilver Messenger Service, the Steve Miller Blues Band, Big Brother and the Holding Company and Creedence Clearwater Revival had all scored high on the *Billboard* charts, creating a local six-million-dollar industry which began to rival Nashville with its productivity and its singleness of image.

Despite the co-existence of nearly five hundred bands, recording facilities were still remarkably provincial. Though Ralph Gleason was to count "eight major studios" in the area, the leading one, Coast Recording at 960 Bush Street, which was eventually converted into the music club known as the Boarding House, still ran on only four tracks.

The search for a more progressive sixteen-track studio was left in the hands of Bill Thompson, who ran down every recording studio in the area. Wally Heider's was really all there was around.

For years Heider, who had been a lawyer in Oregon, had run a remote recording business of the big bands in the 1950s from his station wagon. Eventually he opened a recording studio on North Cahuenga in Hollywood. Now, in the spring of 1969, he decided to expand to San Francisco. The problems in setting up the facility were nearly insurmountable since the zoning ordinances still reflected the antipathy of the local officials to the hippies, who were strongly associated with the music business. As a result, the only locations available were highly undesirable areas out of the ear range of straight residents. "They stuck the studio in a skid row area next to a methadone clinic," said Grace. "There were bars on the other three corners of the intersection."

Long before the studio officially opened its doors, Bill Thompson and Paul Kantner took the grand tour. "I think the carpenters were still there when they first walked through," recalled Ginger Muse, Heider's assistant. Of course the place had every strike against it. Not only was the neighborhood unsafe but the drug addicts of the Tenderloin convened on the very spot looking for an easy hit. The equipment was untested; the facility untried. There was every reason to reject the recording studio and to keep going down to L.A. The Airplane nevertheless was the first band to sign up.

Volunteers was the first major album recorded at the Wally Heider's Recording Studios; Crosby, Stills and Nash, the Steve

Miller Blues Band and Big Brother and the Holding Company booked in soon afterward. The recording schedule at the studio was well-suited to the erratic perfectionism of the Airplane. "They'd start drifting in around six in the evening when I was leaving," said Ginger Muse, "and they'd still be there when I came in at nine the next morning." In fact, the janitor got so used to finding Grace sleeping on the couch in the control room that he simply vacuumed around her.

Despite the surrounding dangers, Grace was never mugged, raped or even propositioned down on Hyde Street coming and going to and from the studio. "After a while, I quietly wondered if I should get insulted." Along with the guys, she always parked her Aston Martin in the "No Parking" zone because it was right in front of the studio door. "I must have gotten over two hundred tickets, but I figured my life was worth it. Once I even left a whole phonograph ensemble in the car and forgot to lock it. It must have been down there on Hyde Street around five hours but nobody took a thing. I figured that they thought nobody in their right mind would leave that much hardware in an unlocked Aston Martin. They were right." The other musicians used to leave their Porsches in the "No Parking" zones and nothing ever happened to their cars either, even if they forgot to lock them. "Once Paul drove a Volkswagen down to the studio, though," Grace recalled, "and left the keys in the ignition. Five minutes later, it was gone."

The band rehearsed for the *Volunteers* recording sessions more intensely than they had done for any of the recent albums. "It breezed through so well that I don't even remember doing it," Grace said. One reason for the unusual amount of practicing was the fact that they had to cut down on their touring during the winter of 1969 due to Grace's node operation. "I wasn't allowed to talk for a month," she explained, "but I could play guitar and piano."

Whenever they had time to practice, like before the recording of *Surrealistic Pillow*, things went relatively smoothly in the studio. "It's when we have to do an album right after coming off the road that things get kind of crazy." Except for a brief stretch of concerts starting March 8 in Honolulu, when Paul got busted, the schedule was clear. Every day they got together in the carpeted basement of the big house, which by now was also fully equipped as a sound studio. "Four large overhead speakers hang in one area of the dark but airy room near a small electronics workshop," observed Ben Fong-Torres, who came for a visit for *Rolling Stone.* "In a nearby corner is a four-track tape recorder, while all over the floor are strewn miscellaneous guitars, drums, chairs, and here and there, leftover copies of Airplane souvenir programs."

The album which resulted from this intensive two-month preparation differed from the others. Its overtones were less poetic, more political. The voice of Paul Kantner was now clearly dominant. What inspired the rest of the musicians to follow his direction was the increasing factionalism throughout the country. Student strikes were erupting in every major university from Berkeley to Buffalo, reflecting the highly charged divisions in values between the generations. In this climate of unrest, the experiences of the Airplane, long acknowledged as leading figureheads of the social revolution, took on a high-toned political significance which was captured in their new lyrics. "*Volunteers,*" wrote Don Heckman in the New York *Times,* "differs from earlier Airplane outings in several respects. Kantner's 'We Should Be Together,' a direct call for a community of youth, and Balin-Kantner's 'Volunteers'—actually a 'Revolution' song—lead the Airplane into a surprisingly direct call for political action."

As Paul's political concerns gained dominance in the band, subtle changes began taking place in Grace's lyricism. Curiously, none of the critics picked up on them. Up to this album, her unique ability had been the crafting of her statements through popular imagery. What she did was make complex ideas understandable to her generation.

Her two songs on *Volunteers* are intricate and untranslatable for mass consumption. Though the themes remain the same as earlier ones, Grace is not tuned into communicating with her audience. "I was talking to myself," she admits, "but I wasn't listening to what I was saying."

On the surface "Hey, Frederick" is another attack on the romantic values of the bourgeois. The sexual imagery, however, is
more blatant, bordering on the grotesque. What she previously
achieved through metaphor she attempts to pull off through
shock. The middle stanzas have little to do with the rest of the
song. Through car imagery, she reveals her inability to cope with
the speed of things around her. "I'm saying that I am flying so
high that I know I am going to burn my wings on the sun unless
I slow down." The foreshadowing of her own imagined doom is
explicit when she sings of the "casket," the "car," being "mine."

"So I'm telling myself that I think I'm enjoying the whole life-
style but actually I am going to run up against the wall if I keep
going ahead with it. I am trying to warn myself but while one
half of me is screaming, the other part isn't listening."

The other song is entitled "Eskimo Blue Day." Paul gave it the
title—"It never made any sense to me," she concedes. Through
natural imagery she projects the insignificance of man's pom-
posity and the meaninglessness of bourgeois values. Instead of
developing her statement through popular metaphor, she focuses
it on key statements. One of them—the line which goes "the
human name doesn't mean shit to a tree"—was immediately attacked by the RCA censor. In the same snip, he tried to cut out
Kantner's phrase—"Up against the wall, motherfucker"—in "We
Should Be Together." The band argued relentlessly until the
RCA executives finally gave in. The songs went on the album intact, proving a major triumph of the San Francisco hippies
against the New York corporation.

In November when the album was released, Janis Joplin, Santana and Creedence Clearwater all had albums in the top 10 of
the Billboard charts. Though the Airplane earned a gold album
with *Volunteers,* it never rose higher than number 13. "In some
ways [however] it may be the most successful of the Airplane
ventures," wrote Ralph Gleason, "since it accomplished what it
set out to do both musically and with the lyrics."

Though the album was conceived more than six months
earlier, it picked up the tenor of the times and set the tempo of
the political rebellion still gaining momentum. On November 15

the songs on *Volunteers* aired on FM radio, underscoring the anti-war March on Washington. It also foreshadowed the growing political tensions of the upcoming Chicago Seven trial. Still, amid the tear-gassing of the students and the silent tyranny of Richard Nixon, Grace was living day by day in a state of optimism. "It was after Woodstock," she said, "and I was feeling a joyous naïveté; an assumption that the misuse of the adrenaline in man could be changed by simply changing man's thinking. I really believed it at the time. I thought that Woodstock proved it. What was naïve was my refusal to accept human nature for what it is. People kill each other all the time. Woodstock was a beautiful fluke. Altamont was my trip back to reality."

As soon as they resettled in San Francisco to record, the Airplane started showing up at Golden Gate Park for free concerts. They played at the People's Park benefit at Winterland and helped Bill Graham net seventeen thousand dollars for the Berkeley Street people. They joined the Grateful Dead for a weekend at Winterland and challenged them to baseball games on Saturday afternoons. The Airplane's team with friends and extended family covering the bases was the Giraffes. The Dead named their team the Dead Ringers. Grace, who had been a cheerleader in high school, revived her old routines, "and cheered once again from the sidelines," according to Thompson.

In between innings, Spencer and Jorma started kicking around an idea they had been talking up for years. "A kind of Woodstock West," Spencer clarified. "We wanted to throw a free concert with the Dead in Golden Gate Park where the Rolling Stones could play too. Not only would it be great for us because we got it together but also for the Stones. Next to the Beatles they were the biggest rock and roll band in the world, and we wanted them to experience what we were experiencing in San Francisco."

The idea gained momentum and finally ended up pretty much in the hands of the Dead. "By the time all the final things were going down," said Spencer, "we were already on the road. The Dead were back home so they ended up putting it together. It was their ball game."

Thompson got the blow-by-blow on the telephone down in Florida, where the band was performing in December. "When we left it was all set," said Paul Kantner. "It was going to be big, a Woodstock West at Golden Gate Park." By the Thursday before the event, December 4, the plans broke down and the whole thing began to become chaotic. "The Stones had agreed to come to San Francisco but the people setting the things up were hassled by the city and police departments." The long-smoldering antipathy between the hippies in Haight-Ashbury and the police came to a head. Now the police sought revenge for the razzings of the past few years.

"I got a call two days before the concert that we couldn't get the permit for Golden Gate Park," Thompson said. The day before the concert the location was still unsettled. Initially it was to be Sears Point Raceway but the owners wanted one hundred thousand dollars in escrow from the Stones. And Mick Jagger hadn't gone to the London School of Economics for nothing.

Not even the flexed muscle of lawyer Melvin Belli could force the Raceway to open its gates. Less than twenty-four hours before the event, Thompson was receiving calls telling the band to go to Sears Point. Then Bob Carter appeared like the messiah and offered his Altamont Speedway across the Bay in Alameda County for the festival. "They took it out of desperation," said Paul, "which tore the whole thing into chaos. There was no way to control it, no supervision or order. Up to the last minute we thought we were going to Sears Point."

The band flew out of Miami into San Francisco on December 5 with Spencer grumbling all the way. He went crazy when he heard all the last-minute changes and told Jorma that he wasn't going to play. "There was no time to put it together. We couldn't pull this one off." Jorma threatened to quit the band if Spencer didn't stop griping and agree to play. "I just told him to quit because I knew the gig at Altamont was going to be a bum trip."

Grace remained sanguine about the whole thing. "I was still looking forward to it. Last-minute changes never bothered me. That's the fun of being in a rock and roll band. I never knew what to expect and I found the confusion both interesting and exciting."

Jorma and Spencer fought throughout the flight. "We hadn't gotten any sleep," Spencer explained, "and we were all very tired."

"I wasn't tired," Grace said. "I felt pretty sure everything was going to work out."

They landed around 3:30 A.M. "Nobody had any time to sleep," said Spencer, "because we all had to meet Thompson at the Embarcadero at 7 A.M. to catch a helicopter to this place Altamont." Nobody had any idea where they were going.

Though the eternal optimist on the flight in, upon landing Grace finally took her prescription sunglasses off, admitting: "The vibes were bad. Something was very peculiar, not particularly bad, just real peculiar."

The day was cold even for northern California in December—maybe thirty degrees. "It was that kind of hazy, abrasive and unsure day," she said. "I had expected the loving vibes of Woodstock but that wasn't what was coming at me. This was a whole different thing."

Chip Monck, who was so instrumental in setting up Woodstock, had labored all night to get the thing together. The equipment was brought in. The stage was set up. "Once again," Grace remarked, "they forgot the toilets." It wasn't surprising this time, however, since nobody really knew what was going on. "In twenty-four hours," Ralph Gleason wrote on December 8 in the *Chronicle,* "we created all the problems of our society in one place: congestion, violence, dehumanization."

Gleason laid the burden of blame on the Stones. "The gathering was religious, of course, which is no new comment, but the high priests were as cynical as any Elmer Gantry." Grace added: "Woodstock had been a joy of new rebellion. The radicals were going to take over and everybody in the bands and audience was equal. We were all doing the same things together. Altamont was the realization that the radicals had tasted the caviar and driven the Rolls. The bands were up on a throne and the Rolling

Stones were holding the scepter. We had so much money that all
of a sudden we realized that we weren't hippies any more. We
weren't drinking beer and smoking joints like at Woodstock. We
were doing a lot of cocaine and expensive drugs. It was a long
distance in five months from Woodstock, from sun to moon, from
good to evil, from marijuana to cocaine."

According to Gleason: "The name of the game is money,
power and ego . . . The Stones didn't do it for free, they did it
for money, only the tab was paid in a different way. Whoever
goes to see the movie [later entitled *Gimme Shelter* and released
in 1970] paid for the Altamont religious assembly."

In many ways the Stones were not the real villains of the day.
"Perhaps it was our naïveté," Grace said. "We invited them to
share the experience of being hippies but we didn't meet them
before, we didn't hang out together and rap about the way
things were. We left it up to the managers. How was Mick
Jagger supposed to know how it was at Woodstock? Nobody had
bothered to show him how things were in San Francisco.

"So the Stones just played it the way that they were used to
doing stuff. They weren't trying to rip us off. They just weren't
from San Francisco and Mick Jagger wasn't a hippie. Maybe he
would have become one for the day if somebody had told him
how it was supposed to be. But there was a definite communication gap."

According to Ralph Gleason, Mick Jagger had contemplated
throwing the Airplane off the program due to the fact that
"they'd outplayed the Stones in Miami. He eventually insisted
there be several groups between the Airplane and the Stones'
performance," Gleason wrote.

The Airplane was unaware of Jagger's strategies as they heli-
coptered into Tracy Airport around eight in the morning. It was
between seventy-five and eighty miles east of San Francisco.
"When we landed there, another helicopter picked us up and
took us to the site," recalled Spencer. "From the air we could see
all the highways had been totally blocked by people parking on
both sides of the road. So no car could get through and massive
congestion resulted. The highway patrol were all over the place."

"Woodstock had been organized badly," Grace said, "but at least it had been organized. As we walked toward the stage at Altamont, chaos reigned." It was a weird red dusty day. "The sunshine never came out, and it was much worse than rain. It was muggy and we were in the middle of nowhere. There weren't any trees. It was dry and ugly. It was a California wheat field."

They had to walk a long distance through a bunch of people to find there were no dressing room facilities. "Somebody had forgotten to put them in. There were too many people on the stage," Spencer said. "Some guys were trying to film the damn thing and other guys were threatening them if they turned on their camera. Everybody was stoned; but it wasn't groovy like in the Park. Fights were starting to break out. People were arguing."

The Hell's Angels were playing security guards to the more than three hundred thousand dispersed in the fields. "They had always been very good at being our security guards for our free stuff in the Park," Grace said. "They never hurt anybody; they just hung around and got drunk and wore black jackets. I think what happened at Altamont is that they decided to really whoop it up. It happens to everybody I know: they begin doing alcohol or cocaine or whatever, then end up taking all of them. It screws up your brain something fierce. Since those guys are aggressive anyway, they would just start stepping on your face. It was probably nerve-racking for them to watch over so many people. It frightened them. And fear raises adrenaline. It all seems physically and psychologically very predictable.

"The first Angels I saw were roaring drunk. They were falling around laughing, and I started laughing with them, too. It was perverse humor like, 'Hey, look at that guy. He just fell off a twenty-foot trunk.'"

The Airplane went on stage second, after the Flying Burrito Brothers. Marty was up front singing. He looked down and saw some Hell's Angels beating up on this big, fat, naked guy who, according to Jacky, "was obviously fucked up. They were beat-

ing him with pool cues and Marty jumped off the stage to protect the guy, who eventually got killed."

"Marty was a street kid but he wasn't into fights," said Grace,
"so I figured that one of the Angels must have challenged him."
What apparently happened was that Marty shot a "fuck you" at
an Angel. To retaliate, "because nobody says 'fuck you' to an
Angel," the Angels decked him.

Spencer, who was playing the drums in the background, was
in shock. "All of a sudden a body goes flying across me on stage.
I didn't know what was happening but I just kept on playing."

Grace was on the other side of the stage "so I didn't know
what was happening with Marty," she said. "Paul used to jump
off stage into the audience all the time during our gigs so I didn't
think anything was wrong because Marty did it, though I wondered why he didn't come back to do the rest of the song."

Grace kept right on singing though she could hear people
yelling at each other. "It wasn't heroic. We were just finishing
the set. If you're still able to stand up, you finish the set."

Besides, "I couldn't see what was going on in the audience. All
I saw were shuffling bodies so I said 'easy, easy' to try to cool
things down." As Paul grabbed the microphone, she remarked:
"It's getting weird up here." A moment later, a Hell's Angel
jumped on stage in response to Paul's sarcastic blast at the Angels for beating up Marty. As the two got into it, Grace tried to
break the tension. "Ya gotta keep bodies off each other unless
you wanna make love."

Fighting spread. Sticks were used. Grace remained on stage
finishing the set. Afterward, Jacky remarked that she had sure
acted brave. "Why shouldn't I?" she retorted with candor. "I had
no idea what was going down in the audience. I couldn't see a
thing in front of me. I had forgotten to put in my contact lenses
that morning."

17

The starched white invitation arrived in the mail addressed to Mrs. Gerald Slick. "The moment I opened it, I knew it was something I definitely ought to attend," Grace said. It was an afternoon tea on April 24 for Finch College alumnae at the White House, sponsored by Tricia Nixon. "And I figured out the perfect escort," she said. She opened her address book and dialed Abbie Hoffman.

The two weren't tight friends—more like spiritual comrades. "We got together for the first time several months earlier when the band was playing around the Washington area. It was kind of inevitable that we would meet since we had so much in common—especially disillusionment with the United States Government. I don't remember who got us together or when we first met but pretty soon afterward Abbie and his wife, Anita, and Paul and me went out for the day to see the historical sights in Gettysburg, which seemed like a perfectly logical thing for the four of us to do. You see, Abbie loved this country. He just didn't like the direction in which it was going. He wanted things to go the way they were originally meant to go, toward freedom for *everybody*.

"The four of us just plopped around Gettysburg making snide remarks under the drone of the loudspeaker giving historical information. Abbie had a real good sense of humor—like a combination of all the Marx Brothers having joined the hippie movement. He was also interested in music. He used to write stuff and sing it to me over the phone but it was kind of hard for him to record any of his songs, especially after he went underground.

"After that trip to Gettysburg we would occasionally phone

each other to find out what was going on. When I phoned him about escorting me, he accepted immediately. I thought he was a good enough performer to put this over on Richard Nixon."

In the weeks before the event, while the band was gearing up for a cross-country tour, Grace was plotting for espionage at the White House. "I wasn't as interested in Tricia Nixon as I was in her father," said Grace. "I wanted to make it rather obvious to the American people that the old man was not wrapped too tight. I wanted to put him to the acid test.

"If you've got a lot of confusion inside your head, acid is going to throw an entirely new light on your behavior. I was not looking to poison the guy. That would have made him a hero like Kennedy or Lincoln. I did not want to make him a legend. The only thing I wanted to do was show America that the guy was just not happening."

A few days later, Mrs. David Busby recalls receiving a phone call from Grace (who coincidentally had been her suite mate at Finch). "Grace wanted to give me the name of her escort and I explained to her that the husbands of the graduates would be given a tour of the State Department during the tea. I asked her if her escort would be interested in this. She said he would and gave me the name Leonard Haufman. This made no impression on me," she said. "It didn't occur to me it was Abbie Hoffman. I just wrote down the name and listed it with the others that I was sending in for clearance by the State Department. I said to her, 'Gee, I hope to see you' and that was that. I didn't give it too much more thought until one of the other Finch women suggested I drop her name from the guest list. She felt Grace Slick was not the sort of girl we would want at a Finch College tea but I told her she was all wrong about Grace. Grace Wing had been my suite mate. And if there was one thing I felt sure about it was that she was much too nice a girl to ever do anything nasty . . ."

The morning of the tea Mrs. Busby got an unexpected call from the White House. "They asked if I could come over *very* early and I said, 'Sure: what's the problem?' The security guard answered: 'The problem, Mrs. Busby, is Grace Slick.'" According to the White House, Grace had called a press conference that morning for the New York *Times,* AP and UPI. There she had announced that she and Abbie Hoffman were going straight to the White House. Grace does not remember calling the media together. "Why would I have done that?" she asks rhetorically, "when I wanted to surprise Richard Nixon?" (In fact, Arthur Schatz, a photographer for *Life,* had heard about the plot and tipped them off.)

"So many of the girls had warned me about her," Mrs. Busby said. "They warned me and warned me and warned me." Putting on her white kid gloves and yellow jacket and dress, she drove to the White House to meet with the security police. "They were very nice, I must say. Mrs. Nixon and Tricia were willing to have Grace come but they were not willing to have her with an escort —any escort—let alone that one."

Around 2 P.M. the rain started. It was a simple drizzle through inclement skies. "Because of Grace, the police had decided to check identifications of all the women," said Mrs. Busby, "so the alumnae were forced to stand in line in the rain. Some of the girls had come dressed up in their best outfits with cute little handbags which really weren't big enough for their wallets, so they weren't carrying any identification. When the police approached them, they had to turn around and look for other girls who had gone to classes with them to identify each other. Some had graduated as many as twenty years earlier so nobody recognized them.

"Everybody was getting furious"—as the rain continued to come down—"and the police must have inspected as many as four hundred women before they got to Grace."

She and Abbie were driven down to the White House from her hotel with Paul in the car waiting. Hoffman was wearing an uncharacteristically conservative suit, white shirt and tie. His hair which had been cut in the Cook County Jail before the recent trial of the Chicago Seven, was short and slicked back. "He looked like a pimp," Grace said.

Grace had dressed in high-class duds: leather boots and jacket, purple midi-length skirt and a see-through black crochet top with pockets over the breasts which Mary Beth Busby, for one, described as "absolutely outrageous. She was obviously not trying to hide anything because it was the kind of net with really big holes and she had on no bra. She didn't look ugly or anything but she certainly didn't look like anybody else going to that tea."

Grace had filled the right-hand pocket of her jacket with powdered LSD. "It was loose and I planned to reach in for a pinch of the stuff when I got Richard Nixon alone in a corner. I figured everybody at these kinds of functions stands up sipping tea and some men and women gesture a lot—enough to sprinkle some powder in his cup. I thought he'd never notice it because you can't see or taste it. After I had done my flamboyant act, I would excuse myself, and around twenty minutes later he would probably excuse *himself* because he wouldn't know why the walls were suddenly dripping."

Instead, the security police nipped Nixon's acid trip in its bud. They led Mrs. Busby down to make the identification "and I told Grace she could come in but Mr. Hoffman was not invited. I had already turned away husbands, brothers, fathers and even mothers and sisters of alumnae.

"Grace told me that she never went anywhere without her bodyguard, Mr. Hoffman," Mrs. Busby reported. "I assured her that this was the White House and they had very good security but Mr. Hoffman interrupted. 'I wouldn't let Miss Slick go in there alone,' he declared. 'I understand they lose a President every three years. It's a dangerous place.'

"'In that event,'" Mrs. Busby concluded, "'if you feel so strongly about it we can't let you come.'"

Once they realized that they were not going to pull it off, both Grace and Abbie left. Mrs. Busby saw them run across the White House lawn and disappear down the street. "I heard something about him draping an American flag made by his wife over the fence around the White House," she said, "but I didn't see him do that."

"Me either," Grace dittoed, "and I was right with him."

When Mrs. Busby finally drew a deep breath and went inside,

she was urged frantically by the social secretary to go back and find Grace. "Mrs. Nixon and Tricia really want to meet her."

Mrs. Busby dashed back into the rain but to no avail. Grace was already out of sight. "We would have been glad to have had her attend the tea, too," Tricia confirmed, "without her bodyguard, quote unquote. If she had to come with a bodyguard I feel sorry for her. She must be really paranoid."

Richard Nixon did not attend the function either, explained Grace sarcastically; "He had probably heard I wasn't coming."

18

Spencer married Sally on January 26, 1970, at the big house. The minister who performed the ceremony was the Reverend Scott Beach of the American Humanist Institute and director of the Committee Theater. Grace was matron of honor.

There had been a lot of people around who had been wondering after a while if Grace and Sally weren't more interested in each other than in Spencer. "They had this strong attraction to one another," observed one of the women living in the big house. "You could feel the chemistry between them."

Spencer found this rapport between his women uncomfortable at best. "But after Grace began going with Paul it was a lot more natural between all of us," he said. By the time of the wedding, the roles were more or less intact. Grace gave them a thousand dollars as a wedding gift, stood up for Sally during the ceremony and attended the reception with around three or four hundred other guests. "It looked like we invited every freak in San Francisco," Spencer said. "Sally and I did not know most of the guests."

The crowd was too much for Grace, who left shortly after the reception had begun. Spencer, for one, was surprised. "She didn't say goodbye to us," he recalled. "She went home to Sausalito with Jerry. She didn't even say goodbye to Paul."

Kantner was preoccupied at the time Grace was leaving. As best man he had stood up for Spencer during the ceremony. Afterward he had gone upstairs to his room and gotten a silver platter covered with a mixture of cocaine and sunshine to be snorted through a hundred-dollar bill. He walked down the stairs carrying the tray to Sally and Spencer as his blessing for the couple. "Only Paul would have thought of that as our sacrament," Spencer said.

Fifteen minutes after the three of them snorted the stuff, Spencer and Sally excused themselves and went upstairs to lie down on the big bed. Forty-five minutes later, Paul knocked on their door. "He was looking for Grace," Spencer said. "I told him she had gone home with Jerry." He disappeared. Twenty minutes later, he knocked again. "He wanted to know if he could sit there with us for a while. We were all stoned on the sunshine. None of us had been aware how strong the stuff was. We were so stoned that Sally and I couldn't go back down to our own reception. We could hear the thump of the music and the video camera working and the conversation, but we couldn't go down and be part of it."

Paul remained with them for at least another half an hour. "He was rambling about Grace. He kept asking Sally why she had gone back to Jerry. I told him that Grace was crazy. You could never tell what she would do or why she did anything. But he wasn't listening. He just kept on saying how much he missed her. He had his head in his hands and you could tell he was in pain. He kept telling us how much he loved her."

A few minutes later, Grace received a phone call from Sally asking her to come back to the big house. "Paul had taken too much acid and wanted me with him. I thought this was really weird because nobody had ever looked upon me as an earth mother." But that night Paul fell in love with her. "I figured," she said, "that the acid twisted his brains."

In a short time Grace gave up her house in Sausalito, and Jerry, and moved to the second floor of the big house as her permanent address. "The benefit of being with Grace was intellectual stimulation," Paul said, "but we still lived on separate floors in the big house to give each other our own space." Nevertheless, they were more or less monogamous.

In May, the band returned to the Fillmore East. Back in Paul's room at the Sheraton Motor Lodge after the show, Grace said that she would like to have his child. "She didn't ask me," Paul recalled. "She just told me that she was going to do it. I was intrigued but I didn't care if she did or didn't."

Grace had given this pregnancy a good deal of thought. "I figured that Paul and I were so opposite in every respect that the child we would create would probably be a rather interesting individual. And it wasn't as if I was imposing fatherhood on Paul, because I had enough money to take care of a child myself and there were plenty of people always around the band so the child would never get bored or lonely. Paul was agreeable and only too happy to do anything he could."

In June, the band went over to Europe to play at the Bath Festival in England. "Things were going fine," said Bill Thompson, "and I was feeling right on top of everything when Grace happened to remark in the car in London: 'Oh, by the way, I'm pregnant.'"

Things had not been running on course for Bill Thompson for months now. At the height of its success, when *Volunteers* was being talked about as the outstanding album of the year, the band was falling into a critical period of dissolution Spencer had been fired in March. "I had already quit about twenty-eight times," he said, "but this time they took me at my word." Joey Covington, a local drummer who had been doing non-Airplane gigs with Jorma and Jack around town, was slated as his replacement. "Look at it this way," Covington told Spencer. "They've asked me to play and I've accepted. Basically what you need is rest."

"Nobody else would give me a straight answer," Spencer said. "Marty kept looking at the floor after they told me. Paul just said that was the way it was. Grace didn't say a word."

"At the time I thought it would be best for him and the band to move on," she said. "I guess it hurt a little bit."

Spencer was admittedly upset and confused but "in a way I figured they were doing me a favor. They thought I was too weak to take the rigors of the road. To them I was just a piece of extra baggage."

With Spencer gone, Grace and Paul decided to move out of the big house. "With the child coming, we wanted to get our own place on the ocean. Paul always wanted to live on the water and I thought it was a good idea." There weren't many residential ports and no homes on the beach in San Francisco. So it was logical to look for a place on the water in Marin County.

The two-story, four-bedroom, one-swimming-pool fantasy they unearthed on the ocean in Bolinas satisfied them both in different ways. "I'm very big on views," Grace explained, "and he's very big on water." Once a nightclub-bordello, it was now converted into a one-hundred-and-fifty-thousand-dollar residence. Through their joint publishing royalties and record sales, they were taking in an annual quarter of a million, "which is nothing next to Elton John but a lot more than we could earn running a one-pump filling station."

Bolinas was a "natural food heaven" where the inhabitants "brushed their teeth with duck grease to avoid the preservatives in toothpaste." Grace was fascinated by these natural food addicts although she admittedly could not always relate to their life-style. "There was this one blond surfer who used to hang out with us and I thought she looked like the sunrise. All she ever did was ride waves with her boyfriend, which was probably very healthy but seemed boring as shit. This other guy was a carpenter and I always considered him an artist in rosewood. They didn't give a damn about rock and roll but they were really into vegetables. They kept telling us not to eat meat because it was a living thing. They made sense but only to a certain extent. They would not listen to reason. I kept asking them why they were eating plants since they were living things, too. They never did answer that. After a while I got to feeling as if I were talking to a bunch of teachers in a parochial school. They were fine as far as they went but they didn't go very far. Since I could not get through to them in any other way, I finally wrote a song entitled 'Cannibal Soup' just to bounce off them."

Back in Wally Heider's studio only two fifths of the band was happening: Jorma and Jack had gone in to cut their first separate album together. "They had started playing in local clubs," said Thompson. "They just liked to play a lot. That's where their thing was at. It used to be in the old days," three years earlier, "that the Airplane would play a concert for two hours and then Jack and Jorma would go to a club and jam till four or five in the morning. I used to have a lot of fun hanging out with them."

Around the Bay Area in the early months of 1970, they picked up Joey Covington and Marty Balin to form a loose quartet. "I could feel another thing was happening with them," admitted Thompson, but nobody wanted to call it a permanent split or the evolution of another band. Airplane was still revved up and flying high in record sales. "I just figured this was something Jorma and Jack wanted to do as a sideline." According to Thompson it was Paul Kantner who casually christened the group Hot Tuna and listened from afar with Grace as Jorma and Jack released their first album in May 1970.

Since the Airplane was not happening, Grace and Paul hung out together in Bolinas with occasional drop-ins by David Crosby. "Both of us liked him a lot," said Grace. "Paul and I were real rigid about stuff. If we were going to sing for anybody —even each other—we have to work it out for six months before doing it. But David was so loose about everything that we really enjoyed him. He used to be able to sit around, play guitar and entertain us."

Steve Elvin, an artist friend, had carved a torture rack for them which "I intended to use as a dining room table," said Grace. "Once when David came over, I strapped him into it." For a while they all just cracked up but as Grace kept on stretching his limbs with the rack, there was about thirty seconds there that he began to wonder how far she would go . . .

Though the house was a romantic fantasy, it was terribly remote from their friends. "We weren't lonely there," she clarified. "We were just perturbed about the distance from the city." In the early days before the birth of their child, "we just laid around enjoying each other, the ocean, beach, pool front, quiet. When I was fat with child I couldn't do anything much except read books and write songs. Most of the time I just spent getting to know Paul Kantner, which is not easy. You have to look hard to see the soft, giving, loving person which is covered by his iron shield."

Sometime during this interlude, Grace wrote a letter to her parents. "It was a long, long, long letter," Virginia Wing said. "It was a lovely, moving letter which said that she was going to have Paul's baby even though they did not plan to get married. She assured us that she had enough money to take care of the child. Naturally I was a little bit upset and Ivan was very upset. I worried a little bit about telling her grandmother, Lady Sue, who I did not think would approve. I did not want to tell her right away but ended up getting on the phone to her the next day." Instead of voicing old-fashioned concern, Lady Sue tried to reassure her daughter. "Don't let it bother you," Virginia recalls her saying. "That Grace is a genius."

Though unmarried and heralded in the media as a liberated couple, Grace and Paul were really quite conventional at this point in their relationship. "We didn't screw any other men or women," she said. "We were just happy with the way it was. Though we were Mr. and Ms. rock and roll, we were quite straight about having a child and living together."

Behind their redwood walls and twenty-foot ceilings—and electronic gate which Paul installed to keep out the hippies who wanted "to stuff banana bread down our throats"—Grace went about getting the house in shape. "David Crosby had a lot of good taste," she said, "and we listened to him a lot. When we told him we wanted to have an extra-king-size bed made, he suggested it be made out of rosewood. So it was." At the foot of the bed, in about two feet of space, Paul stashed his essentials: a pile of his electronic controls for TV and stereo, around twenty science fiction books, a Japanese TV with a half-inch picture, a transistor radio and a brass bowl with brass handles filled with marijuana. He stuck it in their twenty-by-forty-five-foot living room, which he converted into the master bedroom.

With Jorma and Jack doing Hot Tuna, Paul started to conceive his own solo album. "I was busy decorating," said Grace, who had just discovered these Portuguese tiles in a place in San Rafael and ordered around a hundred and fifty thousand dollars' worth of them for Steve Elvin to make into a mosaic in the pool.

Though the tiled pool was a bauble worthy of Hearst's castle, her favorite room now belonged to the unborn child.

There was no talk of marriage preceding the birth of their child. "Why would I want to get married," she asked, "when I was already married?" But around this time Jerry Slick's accountant and lawyer had a heart-to-heart talk with him. "She was just doing too many strange things," he said. A few months before the birth of Paul's child, Jerry sued for divorce.

19

The contractions started coming on at midnight. Paul drove her to French Hospital in San Francisco, where Grace gave birth to a seven-pound daughter on January 25, 1971.

Grace handled her that first day with quiet pride. "China was beautiful," she said. Ivan and Virginia Wing could not have agreed more when they arrived at the hospital a couple of hours after the birth had taken place.

During the labor Kantner had started out in the waiting room but after a while he found an empty room to sleep in. When he finally woke up he went in to see Grace. "He patted her on the stomach," Virginia recalled, "said a few words to her and left. I felt bad for Grace."

Kantner did not come back for the remainder of her three-day stay, "though," he added, "I think I sent flowers." His absence was odd by conventional standards, but Grace says, "it didn't upset me a bit. In the first place, it wasn't his idea to have the baby, and in the second place, he just doesn't like hospitals."

Barely a day after the birth Grace was back in condition; in fact, she was even in rare form. During the afternoon on the first day a nurse brought around "this certificate with a gold star on it," Grace recalled. "She explained that she would write the baby's name on it for me, and then I could take the diploma home and hang it on my wall." To make the nurse laugh, Grace said, "We're naming her god with a small g: we want her to be humble." There was no reaction. The nurse simply left the room and called Herb Caen at the *Chronicle.* The item appeared in his column and was syndicated throughout the country. As Grace was getting ready to leave the hospital, she looked outside and saw a battalion of newsmen. Instead of setting the record straight, Grace confirmed the fact that she had just given birth to g-o-d. The birth certificate, however, read China Wing Kantner.

For the next four months the family settled into a relative tranquillity. "It must have been hard for her living out there in Bolinas, trying to be a mother and having to drive into San Francisco every day to make the albums," said Heidi Howell, who was one of Thompson's staff. "Once people started realizing who they were and where they were living, they began looking in and climbing over walls. They had to increase their security, build a big fence and put up electric doors. They were really isolated. You had to take this winding road all the way up the coast to get there. It took more than an hour to reach them, so not many of their friends used to visit." It was simply a quiet time for both Grace and Paul to get to know their "new small person."

Away from the idyll in Bolinas was the disintegration of the band in San Francisco. "No one was really together," said Thompson, "but the musicians were so polite to each other, they never said no I don't want to work with you. Instead they said sure I'll do it but first I have to do this. It took a year and a half for us to realize it wasn't working."

Marty by this time had faded far into the background. Starting around June 1970, he just wasn't around much. "Nobody really wanted to get together," he explained. "One time there was an odd split. Grace and Paul told me I could get rid of Jack and Jorma and they'd work with me, and Jorma and Jack told me I could get rid of Grace and Paul and *they'd* work with me. So I figured it was time for me to go.

"There was one other factor that made my decision to quit, too. It was the last tour, that last gig on November 27, 1970, in the Fillmore East. We walked out on stage and the people were just standing up, cheering. We hadn't done anything yet. It was ridiculous. There was no challenge for me any more."

"He had been talking on and off about quitting for a long time," Thompson confirmed, "but he got real drunk one night and almost fell off the stage on the last tour. Half the time he was so drunk he could barely stand up. The other half he sang better than he ever had before."

What pushed him over the brink was the death of Janis Joplin, which he blamed on the pressures of her career. The two had never been romantically involved ("She was like a dynamo, very tough, like a man"), but they shared confidences and emotional insecurities sitting around drinking together. "I knew Janis a lot better than I knew Grace. We had more times together," he said. On the night of her death, October 5, the band was scheduled to perform a live television broadcast on channel 9 with the Dead and Quicksilver Messenger Service. "Marty didn't want to go on," Thompson recalls. "He was too broken up about Janis. It really hit him hard."

After that his instinct for self-preservation increased. "I wasn't going to let the same thing happen to me," he said. "I wasn't going to let the pressures kill me. I figured I better get out of the Airplane while I was still alive."

The vibes were not good and the trip was getting destructive. "It was ugly," confirmed Jacky from the front lines in the office. Thompson adds: "It got to the point where Jack and Jorma turned up and played as loud as they could with Paul. They just drowned out the singers, which pissed off Marty. He got very disillusioned and very uptight. Everybody was on their own ego trips. When Hot Tuna started happening, Marty quit."

For nearly a year and a half the band had not recorded together; but in December 1970 the musicians started work on a new album later entitled *Bark*. The sessions were painful for Grace. "No one was connecting. It was like we had brought one musician in from Iceland, one in from New Zealand, one in from San Francisco, another from Outer Mongolia, and none of us was speaking the same language. Everybody was playing in their own dialects. It could have been interesting if we wanted to produce chaos," she said, "but it wasn't the easiest or best way to make music."

The musicians were not working together; in fact, on some tracks they were working counterproductively. "They'd just go in separately and lay down their tracks," observed one of the musicians in the studio. "They weren't relating to one another musically—or any other way." Grace tried to bridge the gap with Jorma and Jack, for whom she had great fondness, through humor. When that wasn't successful she worked on alcohol.

Her songs on the album were reflections of her present state of mind. "Law Man," which was recorded on April 13, 1971, was a translation of her own confrontation with the police. "Crazy Miranda" poked fun at women's libbers.

The pressures were beginning to get to her in May, and she was drinking heavily. "I thought I deserved to get loaded if I was going to continue to be in this business," she explained. "I was supposed to be pleasant in interviews, write music, sing the music, make records and bring up China all at the same time. If I was going to continue to do all these things I needed to take my brains somewhere else in whatever form of 'transportation' I wanted to use."

"Paul did not know how to help her so he just removed himself if she became unpleasant," said Jacky. "It wasn't that he didn't care. He just didn't know how to deal with her."

The band had been more than a professional organization to Grace. "They were my friends. The first people who had accepted me. They were my family. And slowly I saw us becoming the people we were fighting against. At the time we weren't fully aware of what was happening. Jorma only wanted to play by himself. Jack seemed able to go in whichever way he was pulled the hardest. Paul and I were still tying ourselves to the hippie ethic. It was dying right before my eyes. And I was doing everything humanly possible to deny it. I did not want to see my family turning into a business. It was the Roman Empire all over again and this time I wanted to stop it from happening."

The signs were all around her, growing more and more prominent. Thompson was talking about starting their own record company. Paul had turned their home into a sixteen-track recording studio. And as the money stopped rolling into the office, she began to feel pressure about touring to earn the money for her "friends." At home, China was being taken care of by a local girl pregnant with her own child, who also cooked dinner for them. "It was a bad slump," said Jacky.

On May 13 Bill Thompson received a phone call at 3 A.M. Grace had left Wally Heider's studio roaring drunk. Drag-racing home with Jorma, she smashed into a cement wall near the entrance to the Golden Gate Bridge. There was blood all over the area when the ambulance arrived. The attendant had pronounced her dead.

When Bill Thompson got to San Francisco General Hospital, Grace was mumbling incoherently. Her head was wrapped in a blood-drenched towel. Jorma was already there. "If she hadn't been thrown over to the other side of the car by the impact," Thompson said, "she would have been killed." The driver's seat had been totally crushed.

She remained at San Francisco General Hospital for a couple of days, then transferred over to Mount Zion Hospital for a week or two. "She didn't want anybody to come and see her," said Bill Thompson, who didn't go; but Chick Casady, equipment manager, and Jacky Watts went anyway. "When we got there Grace was arguing with the nurses because she was fed up with being in the hospital," Jacky said. "They kept her on heavy sedatives because she kept getting up and moving around. She was supposed to be very quiet because of the head concussion."

While Grace was recuperating in the hospital, Bill Thompson was trying to come up with a cure for the critical condition of Airplane. "Around Christmas I always take off to think about the past year and coming year. But at this point I just kept thinking you can't force people to make music together." Marty was already playing with a group called Grootna managed by Bill Graham. Grace, whose literary bent is obvious in the content of her early songs, had asked Thompson to get in touch with publishers. "She had written a book," said Thompson, "with all kinds of free verse and illustrations." Thompson's lawyer Bill Coblentz recommended various New York publishing heavyweights, and it was eventually Simon & Schuster's Michael Korda who got into it. Thompson delivered the manuscript to him in person. Korda asked that Grace revise it with more of a woman's point of view.

At that point, "she just said screw it," recalled Thompson. "She said she wanted an editor, not a censor." So much for her literary career.

Paul Kantner had gone off on a similar track, only he expressed his political beliefs through a combination of science fiction and music. "We're dealing on levels the establishment doesn't understand. Look at the record collection of any politician and you'll see what I mean. It's like we're talking Greek and living in caves and never coming out as far as they're concerned. They don't know what we're doing so they don't care."

In the fall of 1970 a new album was released entitled *Blows Against the Empire,* a concept album under Paul's direction, with one side entirely a science fiction odyssey and the other a mixture of political exhortations and offbeat ballads. A starship is the locale in the songs on the "Blows" side, and the musicians who put together the record were christened Jefferson Starship. They included Paul and Grace and Jack Casady, as well as Jerry Garcia and Mickey Hart of the Dead, and David Crosby and Graham Nash, among others, comprising some of the key developers of the San Francisco music of the 1960s. The songs consequently took on a special significance, a welcoming of a new decade by the makers of the old.

Through the "Blows" lyrics Kantner and crew reassert their aversion to the establishment but renounce their tactic of confrontation; instead the songs suggest an ethic of escapism which implies a certain resignation to the power and inflexibility of the straight society on earth.

On the non-"Blows" side the voices of Grace and Paul arise in gentle hymns reflecting the present state of their living. "When we did 'Child Is Coming,' we weren't thinking about the birth of China," said Paul in retrospect; but the experiences of their lives nevertheless infiltrate their lyrics. "We were not consciously trying," Grace explained, "but the songs just reflect where we were at that time."

For Grace, Bolinas was a last stop, a hideaway from the changing times, a brief pastoral hangout with "me, him and our child." It was a reclusive haven away from the encroachments of the heavy reality moving in on her. At the same time Jefferson Starship were off in Wally Heider's recording, Bill Thompson was busy renegotiating their future with RCA. "It took me about nine months to get this thing together," Thompson said, "and law students around the world could probably study it for around a year. It was a multi-million-dollar contract—around ten million dollars. Airplane was supposed to do five albums, Hot Tuna three and Paul Kantner three solos with Grace doing one solo album."

On the surface the contract was a financial coup and credit to Thompson and his lawyer, Charles Seton in New York, and to the talent of the band. It worked out fine as far as that went but Thompson unfortunately took it one step beyond that fringe. What Thompson artfully constructed through lengthy negotiations with RCA was a financially complex recording company essentially controlled by the musicians. The Beatles had done it with Apple, and it hadn't worked for them either.

As a business maneuver, Grunt Records, as the company was eventually christened, gave the musicians total control over their artistic products and scored a major victory of the hippies against the strength of the corporate world. "We'd been hassling for years," said Thompson. "On *Jefferson Airplane Takes Off* we had this song called 'Runnin' Round This World' which was vetoed by RCA because it had this line in it about taking fantastic trips. It was a love story, and we intended trips to mean incredible experiences. They took it to mean LSD and cut it right out."

Though it was only the first excision it set a dangerous precedent. When they put this drawing of a "guy's head coming down and around his back on the jacket of *After Bathing at Baxter's*, they made us put pants over the guy's long neck because they said it looked like a dick." The standards for censorship were, as far as the band was concerned, arbitrary and inhibiting to the natural flow of their creativity. "The idea was to form a company," Thompson said, "where the musicians could have complete artistic control, choose their own producers, design their own album covers and record at any studio they wanted."

The contract signaled the creative liberation of musicians from the strong arm of the corporation. "I could go for that," Grace said, but the idea of running their own business turned her off. "That's what really irritated me about the band," said Thompson. "With the exception of Paul, nobody ever took any interest in the record company at all." But, according to Grace, "I never expected Thompson to sing, either."

It was worse than Thompson suspected; the formation of Grunt was a confirmation of Grace's nightmarish fear. "It was the end of the 1960s ethic," she said. "We were becoming *them*."

At the time, however, she went along with it. "A lot of our friends around San Francisco were fine musicians, and we thought maybe we could help them by signing them up and letting them make records with our own company." But as the maxim goes, business and pleasure often don't mix. The first signing to Grunt was Jack Bonus, who recorded an album but "never quite made it," according to Thompson, "because of his attitude." Next came Jorma's younger brother Peter Kaukonen, who was also the husband of Jacky Watts. "That didn't quite work out either," Thompson confessed. Grace and Paul brought in a group named One who performed with a mime troupe in Bolinas. "Their lead singer was a guy named Reality de Lipcrotch who kept coming up with ideas like making albums which disintegrate as you play them so you constantly have to go out to buy more. He also wanted to hold a press conference at the bottom of the Grand Canyon." Thompson said okay. "We'll bring the press down by mule train." Marty wanted Grunt to sign Grootna, the band he had put together and wanted to produce. However, he eventually went with Columbia, doing nothing to alleviate old Airplane hostilities.

The greatest success among the new artists was fifty-four-year-old Papa John Creach, whom twenty-five-year-old Joey Covington had discovered, according to Grace, in a backstreet Los Angeles jazz club. His solo vehicle was entitled *Papa John Creach*, with an all-star backup group including Jerry Garcia, John Cipollina (formerly with Quicksilver Messenger Service), David Brown and Craig Rolie of Santana, and Covington of Airplane.

His funky fiddle was enough of an attraction for a small cult following—the same kind of adulation that Hot Tuna was by then enjoying. Paul wanted to produce an all-girl band called Ace of Cups and Jorma brought in Richard Talbot. "Either Jorma or Paul nixed signing the Doobie Brothers," Bill Thompson recalled woefully. "They were very interested in Grunt. But Airplane wouldn't go for it because they thought they sounded too much like everybody else." So much for commercial judgment.

In its first year of existence Grunt released seven albums which sold more than a million and a half units, which sounds impressive until you realize that this includes the next two Airplane albums, which were instant gold.

The Airplane signed the contract in July. On August 2, 1971, when RCA added its official signature, Grunt Records was born. Several months later, they threw a christening which RCA VP Mel Ilberman is "still trying to forget. I wouldn't exactly call it a party," he said. "It was more of a major event" which cost around thirty-five thousand dollars, which, Ilberman pointed out soberly, "is more than many record contracts."

The happening was staged on the shore in the Friends and Relations Hall, formerly known as the Family Dog, one of the spots where the San Francisco scene started nearly six years before. For a week Papa John's lady had cooked, baked and fried chicken for fifteen hundred people. Fourteen hundred were intimate friends of the group. The main course was really nitrous oxide and cocaine. "God knows," wrote Eric Van Lustbader in *Rock*, "there were enough freaks at the Grunt Gala and they (bless them!) were one of the sources of the evening's success." One hundred square fogeys of the press whom Grunt had flown in and put up in high style at the Jack Tar Hotel were also there amid the wine and chicken (for which guests queued up for more than forty-five minutes only to find the cupboard bare). Mel Ilberman recalls a "heavy amount of smoke in the air—and I don't think it was all L&Ms and Marlboros." Drugs flowed as freely as water starting at 6 P.M. at the rear of the hall, where couples were fornicating. Chuck Seton, the sedate New York lawyer who had negotiated the contract with Harry Jenkins of RCA, sat off in a corner in his Grunt tee shirt mumbling legalisms and trying not to feel too out of place and square. Neither Bill Graham, who had originally gotten the Airplane off the ground, nor Ralph Gleason, whom Thompson regarded as a mentor, showed up. And oddly enough, the musicians in the Airplane seemed strangely out of place. "Marty Balin," according to the writer from *Crawdaddy*, "was looking shamefully morose, glumly surveying the scene with the air of a man with a lot to regret." Paul looked bored. Grace showed up drunk and got drunker. "It was embarrassing," Jacky confirmed. "I didn't want to be there," Grace admitted in hindsight, "and I guess I really wasn't."

Amid the carnival-like chaos of freaks and straights and naked babies running wild, there was ten hours of music performed by the acts signed to Grunt. In between, a Fellini-esque mime troupe performed on stage. "By then Grace was going full tilt," recalled Thompson. "She reached her hands up on stage and playfully grabbed one of the mime troupe by the balls."

The parade of talent started off early in the evening with the band called One. "As a band," wrote Lenny Kaye in *Cavalier*, "they have had the interesting idea of building a large enough group (eight pieces) to contain numerous sub-groups, and members click on and off the stage at various intervals in order to give each of these combinations room to shine." It was, in his words, a "module" concept in rock. Jack Bonus followed, accompanying his "lightweight" original compositions—according to Kaye—with the acoustic guitar. Next came the Ace of Cups, known locally as "the Cups," who were San Francisco's own and only all-girl band. Peter Kaukonen next stepped into the spotlight with his heavy metal band called Black Kangaroo. Wrote Eric Van Lustbader: "He plays very heavy rock steeped in British overtones." Hot Tuna was followed by the Airplane, who played songs from their latest album, *Bark*. "They were the last to come on stage," said Jacky. "It was late, maybe one or two in the morning, and by the time they performed Grace was really out of it." She was dressed authentically in an L.A.P.D. uniform with a set of handcuffs dangling from one wrist, the blouse open to the waist with a black and yellow bikini top peeking out. Mad because of what she felt was the band's excessive volume that night, she spoke her lyrics in a whisper. Midway in the set, she stared down at the acidheads in front of the stage and bellowed: "Shut up!"

Around three in the morning Alice Cooper, the Grateful Dead, Quicksilver Messenger Service and Hot Tuna started to jam. "I turned around to say something to Grace," said Jacky Watts, "and she was gone."

In the fall of 1971, Thompson converted the big house into a business office where the nine or ten employees of Grunt worked. "Grace almost never came into the office, and when she did it must have been very weird for her. When she had lived there, it was like a family scene," said Heidi Howell. "Suddenly the house had completely changed." Her old bedroom was now the main office where Bill Thompson and Jacky ran the multi-million-dollar company. "There were filing cabinets, phones, press releases, mailing lists of five thousand, a promotion office, even a comptroller's office. It must have been real spooky to her."

Early on Paul and Grace had told Thompson, "Hey, you take care of business and we'll pick the acts." But as Thompson quickly realized, they weren't even taking the creative end of the company seriously. "They really weren't putting any energy into Grunt," Thompson observed.

Grace was sensitive enough to pick up on Thompson's reaction. "It nearly drove me up a wall." But Grace never opened her mouth and told him how she felt, though she often expressed her antagonism to the whole business operation through her sarcasm. Nobody, however, ever took her seriously. "They didn't listen because they didn't like what they were hearing," she said. Instead of confronting them, she withdrew. "If people are not listening how can you talk to them?"

Through the bottle she was able to obliterate the things about the reality now that she did not want to see. For business was not only uninteresting to her; it was repulsive. "I had been a hippie before it became popular," she said, "and I didn't make up the word, either. The ethic of the 1960s just legitimized my feelings." As the idealism of the era dwindled, she saw, when she was sober, that the whole ethic was not working. "The beautiful dream of brotherhood and hedonism just came down to the same old shit. I knew if I was not making money, if I was not this thing called Grace Slick, 50 to 90 per cent of my friends would not be talking to me."

There was no question of getting out of the scene, however. "Where would I go?" she asked herself rhetorically. "These are the only people who could be around somebody as crazy as me for any length of time."

20

Grace got busted in Akron, Ohio, on August 21, 1972, booked on assault for pulling a whistle off the chest of a police officer.

"The cops were very uptight," explained Bill Thompson, who was an eyewitness on the scene. "They maced a bunch of kids throwing rocks at them and the tear gas choked the band on stage." The Airplane cut short the concert at the Rubber Bowl and the crew came on stage to pack things up. Chick Casady was moving equipment when he saw some cops beating up the kids dancing in the aisles. He yelled at the cops, "Why don't you pigs leave those people alone?" They were on him in a second. They handcuffed him and gave him a bloody nose.

Backstage Grace saw them carrying him off. She ran over to check what was happening and a patrolman, according to Thompson, who was watching on the sidelines, "pushed her aside. To stop from falling backward, she grabbed his police whistle. The cop slugged her in the face and gave her a black eye."

Paul rushed over to defend her. "He jumped on that one cop and wrestled him to the floor. But two other cops jumped him and slammed his head against the ground."

The three spent the night in jail until Thompson came up with the five hundred dollars bond. Upon release, Grace was rushed to Akron City Hospital and X-rayed to find out if her nose was broken. As it turned out, the black eye was the only injury. Though she was obviously shaken up from the incident (it was the first time she had personally gotten busted), she never did admit being upset by it. "At the time I figured if I got my face messed up in one of these riots they could always give me some drug to get rid of the pain and a plastic surgeon could either put the same face back or a new face on."

Two days later at the Auditorium Theater in Chicago, Grace was acting kind of weird before the show. "She was fucked up on something," confirmed Thompson, "and in one of those moods where I never know what she is going to pull next." Decked out in a black nylon floor-length skirt, transparent puckered shirt and the black eye she had picked up in Akron, "she also looked a little, well, just a little . . . wrecked," wrote Beth Lester in *Creem*.

She got through a raucous singing of "Somebody to Love," then the monitors faded out. "Sing 'White Rabbit,' Gracie," shouted someone from the audience. "I can't," she retorted, according to Lester; "it's not on the set list. The blond Nazi on my right makes up our list. He never tells me. I don't know what's going on it until we play it." Clicking her heels and executing a Third Reich salute, she concluded: "What he says, goes."

She was obviously off in a zone but the kid didn't quit. He kept on insisting she sing "White Rabbit."

"It's on the cassette, turkey," she retaliated. "Lay off. That was 1965! Are you still the same person you were seven years ago?"

As Casady and Kaukonen were tuning up for the next number, some punk kid yelled out: "Take off your chastity belt, Gracie!" Grace yanked her black nylon skirt up to her chest and said, "What chastity belt? I don't even wear underpants."

Around eleven the set ended. "The guys all trooped off to thundering cheers (it was a good show) and a certain callback," Lester wrote. Grace stayed on stage, sitting on the floor. She held the microphone between her legs, staring at the audience. "She teased all the guys. She spoke a little about being the girl in the band, about women's libbers in dirty jeans, but still, they did have a point." The audience, by and large, was unimpressed. Stoned on coke and alcohol, her thoughts were disconnected and random. Hardly anybody could follow what she was saying. Finally after seven minutes of extemporaneous flow, she stood up. "I was born here," she said softly. "Isn't that weird? Did you know that? I was *born* in Chicago." She slammed down the microphone and walked off. Thompson told her that she was brilliant; the press reported that she was pathetic. But no reporter ever put together the state she was in and what had just happened to her in Akron.

From the start of this last Airplane tour, Grace was not quite herself, "whatever that is." It was as if she didn't want to be there but was proving too weak to liberate herself. The vibes from Jorma and Jack were ignoring everything, including the music. The shows were mediocre at best, with the cops always showing up in the audience for the finale. When two hundred policemen in riot helmets brandishing wooden clubs appeared at the end of the Airplane's three-hour set for the Nassau Easter Seals Drive, Grace flipped out. "You can't have these cops here during our act," she screamed, leaving the stage. "What is this, Auschwitz?"

The last Airplane tour was proving the cadenza of the era. Already the names and faces of the musicians were changing. Papa John Creach was there, playing impulsively and drowning out the structure of the songs. Joey Covington's "punk WASP" personality had clashed with the other members of the group, and John Barbata, formerly of the Turtles, had taken his place. David Freiberg, who was an old roommate of Paul and a member of Quicksilver Messenger Service, was invited by Grace and Paul to come along. "They knew I was out of work and living on food stamps," he said. "They just phoned me up and told me they would like me to sing harmonies with them since Marty was gone."

On stage the interaction between Jorma and Paul was getting rough. It was as if they were engaging in a sparring competition. Each one was trying to play louder than the other. "I guess they really didn't want to be doing it any more," said Grace in retrospect. "We didn't fully realize it at the time but the only reason we were out there together was to make money."

The friction with Jack and Jorma went on off stage. They teased Grace about her drinking and her weight, which was ballooning up to a hefty one hundred and fifty pounds. The reviewers were calling her Elizabeth Taylor or Mama Cass. Jack and Jorma came up with less complimentary comparisons.

Though Grace parried their stabs with thrusts of sarcasm, she was hurting. The stunts on stage when she was drunk now turned from the provocative to the outrageous. "It was," remarked one musician, "as if she were doing a caricature of her own public image."

On August 13, 1972, underneath the rain clouds in Gaelic Park in the Bronx, a groupie named Sunshine interrupted the stage performance to do a self-styled rain dance in front of the audience. "Let's all take off our tops to stop the rain," she cried; "I'll go first." Grace was second. Thompson almost died. In front of the band before thousands of people, Grace Slick stood naked from the waist up. "She was sucking on a lollipop," Thompson groaned, "while the band was tuning up."

The exhibitionism was out of character for Grace, who had long been more talk than action. In fact, when *Playboy* had once approached her to pose as a centerfold she turned them down flat. "She knew it would kill her father," Virginia Wing explained.

Back in San Francisco, the era formally closed as Grace and Paul moved out of their idyll in hippieville into a high-class neighborhood in the city. Paul had been eyeing this half-a-million-dollar palatial residence for years. It was the only residential property in San Francisco right on the Bay. "At one point he told me how much he wanted that house," said Jacky. "When Grace said the same thing to me, I sent out a letter to the occupants, asking them to contact me if they ever wanted to lease or sell."

Three days later she got a call. "The couple living there was getting a divorce. The house was up for sale."

At the time of moving, Grace and Paul were on the road with the Airplane. The burden of packing up and supervising the movers fell on Pat Dugan, who had joined the family as China's nurse and become Grace's right-hand friend. A burly woman with a rich spirit and maternal warmth, she was raising her own four children herself. They became part of Grace and Paul's clan and a surrogate family for China. "Paul told me we were moving on Friday," Pat recalled. "I was sad because the kids liked

Bolinas. (Grace had bought Pat her own house down the road from them.) But once I saw how excited he was I was more than willing. He told me on Wednesday. It wasn't really frantic—just short-timed."

Paul moved the big bed into his room on the second floor. Grace chose her room at the back of the same floor, decorating it in Moorish, Chinese and San Francisco. "We like to be with each other, so we are in one house," explained Grace, "but we have two different rooms and that helps us keep our individuality. If we didn't have two rooms, we probably wouldn't still be together." By the fall of 1973, they were already leading separate lives. "She liked to snort coke and drink," said David Freiberg, who stayed with them for around a month when his wife kicked him out for falling in love with a female studio engineer. "Paul had stopped snorting and never drank. So she started hanging out with people who did her thing. She hung out at the Cliff House restaurant for a while with me and Mickey Hart [drummer for the Grateful Dead]. She and Paul were taking regular karate lessons twice a week from Byong Yu in Berkeley, and she used to enjoy chopping Mickey, who had a black belt in Judo. He had been an instructor in the Air Force. She didn't frighten him—just everybody else around."

It didn't take much to get Grace drunk. According to Freiberg: "She'd drink Dom Perignon in the dressing room, Blue Nun on the road. In her house it was Kahlua or champagne. She never slurred her words or fell down. She would get very loud and belligerent. Then she would start attacking people. She thought she was being sarcastic but she was too drunk to realize how mean and nasty she could become. She had a strange way of hearing people and she'd misinterpret a remark and come back with something completely off the wall. I remember this one time she got so out of hand that I had to leave. She was too much for me. I went out and sat in the car. I couldn't stand it any more."

Paul was cool. Whenever she got drunk, he ignored it. "He would come home," Pat said, "and she would attack him. She would make really mean comments to his face. He never reacted.

He would listen, then go up to his room and turn on the television."

Her flights into the night were by now recurrent. Paul never tried to stop her. "I could not take responsibility for her," he explained. Pat would sit up half the night with her; "she, Danny (Pat's son) and I would laugh about everything. It probably drove poor Paul crazy but it was good in a lot of ways because it kept her there. At least she was home."

Despite Pat's efforts, Grace continued to flee. "For a long, long time I didn't see much of her," Pat admitted sadly. "She would always leave me notes with drawings on them. I still have some of them."

Most of the time nobody knew where she had gone. Speculating on her whereabouts was a daily game around the Grunt office. But nobody could outguess her. "How could they?" she said. "I didn't even know where I was myself." There were nights at the Cliff House. She and Jacky Kaukonen used to close it down. Other times she would check into the Miako Hotel alone. "I thought they had the best room service in town." Once Pat Dugan came down in the morning to find gashes in the bread board. "Grace had whacked the hell out of it with a Samurai sword."

One night Grace appeared backstage at Winterland as a guest at a Crosby, Stills and Nash concert sponsored by Bill Graham. In the middle of the performance, she broke loose, took center stage and started doing karate forms. "I took her in the back," recalled Bill Graham, "and somebody drove her home. "She called me the next day and did something which I knew was very difficult for her. She told me she was sorry and that she felt bad about what she had done. I told her that I hoped this wasn't just a phone call. I hoped she was going to do something about her drinking."

Around the Bay Area her midnight escapades were fast becoming notorious. Over the next few years, her debauch legend was going national. On the morning before her appearance on Chip Monck's talk show "Speakeasy," Monck sent her a bottle of champagne. By the time she arrived at the theater, she had finished the bottle. According to Thompson: "It was James Taylor, Peter, Paul and Mary, Dr. John and Waylon Jennings. Neither Grace nor Waylon was feeling any pain and they started exchanging bad-mouth quips, and they continued even when the cameras were rolling. For a while it looked like it might get out of hand, but afterwards, they ended up liking each other." Similarly, Geraldo Rivera made the mistake of asking her during one of his straight interviews what it was she had always wanted to be. Candid to a fault, Grace answered: "Blond with big boobs."

The worst hour came in 1974 when Grace terrorized the whole staff of KSAN radio station in San Francisco. "People were fleeing in fear of her," said Thompson, who received a phone call from Tom Donahue, the station's Big Daddy, on the following morning. "Either you do something for that girl," he said, "or you're going to have another Janis Joplin."

Shortly after the last tour of the Jefferson Airplane in August 1972, Jorma and Jack had left the country for a long stretch of speed skating in Scandinavia, leaving Grunt Records on thin ice. "RCA was primarily interested in the albums of Jefferson Airplane," explained vice-president Mel Ilberman. "The company had already lost hundreds of thousands of dollars on its investment in the new Grunt artists. Some of them I think were very fine artists," he conceded graciously, "but while they may have been worthwhile creatively they were not as strong commercially as we would have liked."

The executives at RCA had not wanted to make the investment in new acts; but the band, via Thompson and his lawyers, wouldn't sign without it. When the new Grunt artists bombed, bitter resentment against the band grew up around the corporation. "I think some of those guys really wanted to kill us," said Thompson.

As the failure of the new artists became apparent, RCA began exerting pressure on the Airplane for their next album. "They had been giving us phone calls every day about being on time with the next Airplane album," said Grace. "They kept asking us when we were going to make another record, and I told them whenever Jack and Jorma got off the road with Hot Tuna and came home." The phone kept on ringing. "Finally we just had to tell them that we couldn't make a record until we had a band again."

Around 1973, the money stopped rolling in from New York. According to the contract, funds were forthcoming only on receipts of the albums. No albums, no money. Millions of dollars had already been expended but Grunt Records had dissipated it. "They were living in a style to which no one is accustomed," remarked Ilberman. By 1973, Grace owed more than $62,000 in taxes to the government in one year, but there was no money for paying it. Grunt Records was operating on an austerity budget for supplies. "We didn't even have pencils," said Heidi Howell. "It was a very hard time for all of us."

At that point Grace blamed the lack of good music on the increasing time being spent with the business of trying to run the failing Grunt Records. Thompson blamed Grace and Paul. "They had the perfect vehicle for making a lot of money," he said, "but they never really got involved." They had stopped doing interviews, and they were openly antagonistic to RCA. "They were fighting against themselves," said Thompson, who was missing the obvious point that Grace had never wanted to build an empire in the first place. "When it first started," she recalled, "the whole thing was small. Just a family business. Since I prefer autonomy to making records for a corporation, I thought it was fine to get our own company in San Francisco. But I didn't want to turn into Clive Davis. I didn't want to turn into a cash register every time I looked into the mirror. I was not interested in all the bullshit that goes down with business."

"Grace didn't have the patience for running a business," Ilberman confirmed. "She just wanted to work, live well and not worry about money, but she started running into problems when she needed money and discovered there wasn't any." Most of it had been frittered away or handed out to the extended family of the band. Around her people she considered close friends were hitting her up for money. "Grace always gave it," said one girl friend.

The albums produced by the band during this time reflected the changing ethic of the scene. Though *Bark, Sunfighter,* and *Long John Silver* scored in the top 15 of the *Billboard* charts and earned gold records denoting more than a million dollars in sales, the music was dispirited and the intricacy of blended sensibilities which had been the hallmark of the group was now gone. "Marty Balin is no longer with the group," wrote Patrick Snyder-Scumpy in *Crawdaddy,* "and although his creative role declined steadily since *Surrealistic Pillow,* his voice and the wailing emphasis it lent to the vocals are irreplaceable."

The problems on these albums went deeper than the personnel. "I didn't like the way they were recorded," admitted Thompson. "Paul would lay down a track and then the drummer would lay down a track and then Grace would lay down her tracks. It didn't sound like they had taken any time working together."

Fortunately for the Airplane, the quality of their harmonies was not the only change in the sound of pop music. "Rock has now reached a stasis" in the 1970s, wrote Scumpy, "a plateau of competence. But within it individual artists continue to grow or decline in accordance with the particulars of their situation." By the early 1970s, the voices of rock were indistinct and transitional. "Its temples are filled more with smack, reds and money vultures than with innocence and joy," wrote Scumpy. "Mourn the music. It has died."

Paul Kantner had found a bridge between the sensibilities of the decades through science fiction. His *Blows Against the Empire* brought literary distinction upon Grunt when it became the first musical production in history to merit nomination for science fiction's Hugo Award, in 1970. Though it ultimately lost, it raised anticipation for Kantner's other solo projects and heralded a new step forward by Grace Slick.

Grace had long been looking forward to taking the solo plunge; but the timing was unfortunately wrong. The situation at Grunt had not really improved. Grace's inclination was to get out of the whole damn thing, but loyalties and guilt kept her from getting free. As a result, the drinking which had always been periodic was now becoming excessive. David Crosby took to calling her the Chrome Nun. "She was funny, making jokes, off-the-wall stuff," said the young guitarist Craig Chaquico. "Somebody would say something and she would pun on it. She was very funny, warm—and a little embarrassing. You could tell she was really hurting."

In this condition she went into the studio to create the tracks for her first solo venture. "What she should have done," speculated one of the musicians around the studio then, "was take around a year off and go live in Hawaii. But all her friends were telling her what she needed was to work." (In truth, it was what they all needed to pay the bills.)

Grace was not imperceptive and exactly because she knew what was going on, she kept on drinking. "They didn't see me; I felt like a personality rather than a person." On the one hand, she was ready to walk out. But there was Paul and China. And there were the years of friendship and marijuana in the 1960s which were not so easy to obliterate. As Grace began work on her album, the conflicts raged inside her, and a silent mourning for her generation of flower children now going hard cash.

For the basic tracks she dug up the score she had originally composed for Jerry's film at San Francisco State. She added lyrics and Spanish intonations through the rhythms. "There were words she wanted to be in Spanish as far as the tongue, the flow," said Bob Mathews, engineer in the studio. "So she'd wait around at six in the morning until the Mexican janitor showed up," he said. "Then she'd corner him and ask him to translate her words while he was emptying garbage cans."

Basically the backup musicians on the album were out of the Grunt stable, but there were a couple of exceptions which came as major surprises. Jack Casady played his "roaring dinosaur" bass and Ron Carter, who was one of the best young jazz musicians in the country, played the rhythmically smooth sounds. Jorma had long been recognized as one of the most original lead guitarists in the Bay Area. Finding a replacement for him on this album wasn't easy; but Grace had her eye on a young guitarist, Craig Chaquico, who had not yet graduated from high school. His English teacher Jack Traylor had been one of the artists on the Grunt label. He had been recording his album entitled *Child of Nature* at Wally Heider's in January and February 1973, when Grace, Paul and David Freiberg were working upstairs on their next album, entitled *Baron von Tollbooth & the Chrome Nun.* "David Crosby and Graham Nash were falling in on their sessions," observed Chaquico, who was playing on Traylor's album. "The Pointer Sisters came round and Tower of Power did the horn sections on a couple of cuts. Jorma sat in and so did Mickey Hart from the Dead. I was only sixteen then," he said, "and knocked out by all these Bay Area musicians around."

Eventually Craig drifted into their sessions too and sounded so good that he wound up playing three songs on the album. "On the song 'Fishman' I even traded guitar licks with Jerry Garcia," said Craig, "but I didn't feel like a punk kid. Everyone I met through Paul and Grace—all the musicians on the scene—had this down home friendly attitude, no bullshit, no star trips."

Grace was especially without affectation. It was one of her endearing qualities. She was so self-effacing that it was hard to believe that she was the headliner on the scene. "I mainly remember looking through the window into the control room," said Craig, "and seeing her hanging around just to listen to me. I couldn't believe that she was there just because she liked my playing but then there wasn't anybody else in the studio . . . I didn't want to get my hopes up . . . but then what else was she doing there except listening to me."

When he first went in to record with her, "she got drunk as we worked. Then she'd go turn the guitar up and tell me to make it ballsy. It was just how I wanted to play. She wanted me to make it loud, raunchy. She was very patient with me. She took hours for one song and we'd improvise it through. She couldn't hum the guitar parts but she knew when she heard it and I was inspired by her vocals and sexy lyrics. They gave me ideas to play. I could really feed off her energy and ideas."

By spring when the sessions started for *Manhole,* John Barbata shifted over from the Airplane to her solo album. David Freiberg did similarly and helped Paul and Grace in producing it. Steven Schuster, who had married Ginger and fathered their son

Wolfgang, was asked to write the score and do arrangements. Bob Mathews had been hanging around the studio for a couple of weeks and eventually took over the engineering of the album. "It was a family-type scene," said Mathews, "which is how things happen around San Francisco. Most musicians get to know each other as friends and out of their common interests they become professional associates. That's the way things work here."

The sessions for *Manhole* were held in the evenings when Grace and Paul would show up at the studio. For years Grace was known for her reliability. Despite her lunatic public image, she was always quite disciplined, prepared and professional behind the scenes. She did her homework and arrived on the scene early or on time. Now, however, "she was very much self-abused. She drank too much, smoked too much. She also shared my desire for particular drugs that kept us awake longer and allowed us to do more," said Mathews. "Basically she was very unhappy and I had the feeling I was dealing with a woman who was going down the tubes."

Though she and Paul were working together in the studio, "they were divergent people," said Mathews. "Paul was more settled at this point as far as his music and career. He liked to approach everything in order and Grace was just the opposite. When in doubt she liked to stir things up. She'd do crazy things. Paul dealt with them by ignoring her." As a result, the two were drawing further and further apart. "Grace was starting to hang around people who would go in her direction and liked the same kind of things," said David Freiberg. As the sessions got under way she began spending more and more time with Mathews, who had just separated from his wife Betty, whom David Freiberg had fallen in love with. Around the recording studio, there were Ping-Pong and pool tables. "Grace would come down and play pool with me. It's the only time I was ever paid $15 an hour to play pool for four hours straight. That was the way the situation was at that point," said Mathews.

A few weeks later, Grace found out where Mathews lived and showed up on his doorstep. "There was a part of her which was wanting to be free," said Mathews. "She was doing what felt right at the moment and not having to explain it to anyone but me. She did not feel that there would be any consequences. I provided the ability to be not tied down but still covered in the family."

Though Paul was not oblivious to what was going on (it was happening right under his nose in the studio), he never confronted her with it. "She'd go home around eight-thirty in the morning to spend time with China," said Mathews, "and then she'd go to sleep." The schedule became hectic because in effect through the spring of 1973 she was leading two lives. "So she'd be up all one night and the next night she wouldn't show up at the studio," said Mathews. "Paul and David would take over and do the work."

Despite the loose life-style of rock society, Grace and Paul had been straight with each other for three years or so; but now their differences were mounting. Their life-styles were divergent, "Paul being rock and roll twenty-four hours a day." "The band was around a lot of the time," Pat Dugan said, referring to Paul's and Grace's new house, "because they used to rehearse there." He had converted their enormous living room into their rehearsal hall and put a sixteen-track recording studio into the basement. "There were always a lot of people around," said Pat, a number of them deadpans and hangers-on. "Everybody used to be in Paul's room. So when Grace would come out of her room after a nap, she might be stark naked but she'd always have to go to the bathroom and put on her clothes and make up her face just to wander around her own house."

Grace was basically a private person and the number of people around nearly drove her crazy. By 1973, she had no escape from rock and roll.

Bob Mathews was the logical choice for relief. Though part of the San Francisco music scene, he was one of the few men who was not involved with Grunt. With him she could consequently achieve the freedom from the situation yet not entirely surrender her security. "I had good times the whole time we were recording," said Mathews. "That's why I got involved in her album. Grace is as crazy as I am."

Though she technically had creative control, Grace did not exert her authority. "All she really did was choose the people she wanted to work on it and see what they could do." Adds Steven Schuster: "She could take as much interest in it as she wanted. If she didn't, it would get done because there was always Paul." In earlier days, Grace had stuck around the studio from dawn to dusk totally involved in every aspect of the albums. Now alcohol and cocaine, as well as lack of sleep, were "messing up my brains." Her involvement was erratic; her concentration came and went. "It was very frustrating in a lot of ways because she would change her mind," said Schuster. "It was like one thing one day and another thing two weeks later. I ended up doing three versions of the orchestrations. The original thing had twelve pieces like an orchestra. Then as she got more enthusiastic, she wanted to use more pieces."

One night she walked into the studio and asked Mathews how she would go about adding strings. "She wanted to know the alternatives. I told her we could go to Hollywood like everybody else, or we could go to London. That's where everybody had been doing it for a real long time. Union scale for musicians there is half what it is here."

Four days later she walked into the studio and told Mathews: "We're going to London."

Everybody went. They flew first class on a 747 and booked three three-hour sessions at the Olympic Studios, where the Rolling Stones had done a lot of their early recordings. RCA footed the bill. Back in San Francisco five days later, they did some recording in the sauna at their house. "David Crosby was there that night and I think he changed some of the songs and did a little background singing with David Freiberg and Paul," said Pat Dugan. As the album was evolving on two continents, Grace was losing more and more control. "She was really wasted at times," admitted Steven Schuster, "and it was obvious that she could not cop the whole thing herself."

Side two therefore became a Paul Kantner-David Freiberg production with Grace doing most of the vocals when she would show up. "She was painful-funny in those days," said Schuster, "and you knew she needed help but you didn't know exactly what to do. I wanted to help her and I tried to do what I could, which is to say nothing at all."

As the album came to a finish after close to six months of work, Grace Slick's solo venture turned out to be a halfhearted production. Only half the album was governed by her. Grace christened it *Manhole* "because that's what I was at that time."

Back in New York, RCA was paying the astronomical bills and waiting with bated breath for the product. When it arrived, "you might say that we were disappointed," said Mel Ilberman. "It was not exactly what we had expected." Commercially the album, with a self-portrait of Grace on the jacket, was not a success. The failure increased her insecurity, which in turned added to her drinking.

By Christmas, Bill Thompson knew they were in deep trouble. "At that time I called Mel Ilberman and asked him if RCA would be willing to renegotiate the contract because we weren't making any money." Ilberman listened. Thompson suggested accepting the fact that the musicians of the Airplane were split in two camps. "If we could talk Grace and Paul into forming another band, then we would have two bands and make a lot more money."

Paul would go for it. But Grace, who was still trying to reestablish the original band, said no. "I kept talking to Paul," said Thompson, "but Grace still didn't want to do it." Finally one day Paul called Thompson to tell him Grace had changed her mind. "There were a lot of sad things going on at that time," Pat Dugan observed. "Grace was taking the change badly. She had always thought of the Airplane as her family and she did not want to perform as a band without the others." But circumstances and finances won out. "I can remember Paul and Grace sitting around trying to think of a male vocalist who could take Marty's place. Well, they sat and thought about it," said Pat, "and they could only come up with Mick Jagger, but he already *had* a job."

The nucleus of the new band was already around them. David Freiberg, John Barbata and Papa John Creach had been playing with them on the last tour of the Airplane. Craig Chaquico and Peter Kaukonen were obvious choices, both from the point of musical talent and appearance. The English musician Pete Sears had worked with them on *Manhole*. Now that they finally had a working band, they had to come up with a commercial name. According to Thompson: "They thought about calling themselves 'Paul Kantner and Grace Slick' or something like that, but Paul already had 'Blows Against the Empire' and Jefferson Starship. And that was it."

21

It was the first tour of the Starship. When Grace and Paul arrived back at the hotel after a concert in St. Louis, there were some kids hanging around in the hallways the way they usually do after a show. One girl in particular was very sedate and quite beautiful in comparison with most groupies. She and Grace and Paul began a casual conversation about the show while the rest of the band and crew were coming back sporadically from the auditorium. The chat was pleasant and Paul invited her to come back to their room for a while. "I felt sorry for Paul," Grace said. "I knew that he would have enjoyed spending the night with this lovely lady, but he couldn't do it with me right there in the next room." The girl remained for about fifteen minutes, then politely excused herself, knowing the situation was obviously not going to be the setting of a party. "I watched her go the length of the hall," Grace said, "because I wanted to find out which one of the guys would have the right come-on to entice her to join him. So far none of the band seemed to catch her attention, and none of the crew either—yet." Finally the girl turned into one of the rooms, "but I hardly recognized Skip Johnson." He was a new member of the crew, a light man from the East Coast, and she wondered what it was about him that made the young girl choose him over the rest of the guys. The next morning the five-foot-eleven, hundred-and-thirty-five-pound Johnson came out of his room with a construction worker's helmet on. "With his small frame and long curly black hair sticking out under the hard hat, the joke was obvious, but well executed because he said absolutely nothing about it—no silly remarks, just the hat." That sense of humor appealed to Grace, so she decided to find out more about this fellow who so nonchalantly won the evening's prize.

At the age of twenty-two, Edward (Skip) Johnson had become in less than three years one of the hottest young lighting men around, having worked with Stephen Stills, Dave Mason, Jethro Tull, the Who, and the Doors before joining the Starship tour. Unlike all of the other guys around the band, he was an Easterner. He had grown up in Philadelphia, the eldest of six children. His father, Ed Johnson, was a milkman, his mother Mary a housewife and devout Catholic. Before finishing two years at Bucks County Community College as a liberal arts major, Skip rolled up his sleeves and worked in a car wash, pumped gas as the night manager of a station and finally ended up cleaning toilets in convention centers around the Jersey Shore, where he met Larry Magid, who helped him become stage manager at the Spectrum in Philadelphia.

The band did not go into Wally Heider's to record the first Starship album, entitled *Dragonfly,* until the first of July, when they put down the tracks for Kantner's song "Ride the Tiger," with some lyrics and music by Grace. By then, Maurice Ieraci, who was in charge of production for Grunt of the albums, had hired Larry Cox as the new producer for the group. Cox had come up through the ranks as the drummer of a country and western band once slated to go on the road with Buddy Holly. He had met Paul and Grace years before at Graham Nash's house, where he was working on Nash's album entitled *Songs for Beginners.* "They had just stopped by for a social visit. I didn't know who they were," Cox said. "I was not into hard rock, and I hadn't heard of the Jefferson Airplane at that time." Around three or four years later, he got a phone call from Ieraci. "Since I had no idea who he was I didn't bother to return his call," said Cox, who was then completing a bluegrass album, "but he made a deal with one of the nicer ladies on my answering service to definitely make sure I phoned him back.

"We just tapdanced for around fifteen minutes on the phone, and I wrote down 'Jefferson Starship.' 'Who the hell were they?' And Maurice Ieraci; 'Who the hell is he?'"

When Cox's attorney confirmed Starship's moneyed status in the recording industry, Cox sat down for coffee with Ieraci, who eventually selected the low-key producer from fifteen other candidates. "To this day I can't figure out why he picked me," said Cox, "but I had always made nice-sounding records and didn't rip anybody off. Still, I wasn't much of a rock producer. In 1971 I had produced a group called Climax and the tune 'Precious and Few' went into number one. But I felt sure they must have met a lot of other guys with bigger reputations than that."

Cox did not meet the group until he had agreed to do the album. "It hadn't seemed very important," he conceded. Barbata had worked with Cox on the Nash album and Ieraci liked him. "I also knew none of the history of Airplane," Cox said. "I had no ideas that they had been bananas . . ."

At the end of June, Larry Cox met Jefferson Starship at Paul and Grace's house in San Francisco. "When I walked in, Grace just looked at me and thought: 'Well, here comes Los Angeles.'" But later she told him that she was totally baffled because "she didn't think I talked L.A. or acted that way." She spent the rest of the rehearsal trying to figure out where Larry Cox was coming from.

The first night in the studio, "she immediately tested me," said Cox. "She'd dish it out until you'd stop her and she had found your limit. But she never found my limit because I'd always carry it as far as she would go until she got tired of it."

As the Starship got off the ground, the flight was smooth. Grace was superficially happy that things were jelling but was herself merely a physical presence in the band. At the time she was still trying to "enjoy" the situation through a combination of cocaine and alcohol, but the state of her mind and her recognitions kept infiltrating the lyrics on her albums. "I was telling everybody what I was feeling," she repeated, "but nobody, including me, was listening." The statements were, however, transparent and as clear as any declaration of independence. On the final cut of the first side of *Manhole,* she sings: "Don't tie me down, I want to run, give me the sun. If you see me and you think I'm just about to leave, or dash, you can follow me, but I'm already gone."

A year later, the feelings of isolation had matured into the lyrics for the song entitled "Hyperdrive." "I never thought there were corners in time," she sings, "till I was told to stand in one. One straight line, head-on into the other. Maybe standing in the corner looks like where it's got to come. But I'll pretend one wall is the past and one is the future and I'll stand here like the present looking for a good place to run . . ."

The geometric imagery was inspired by her recurrent readings of Buckminster Fuller. Though the lyrics were complete, they had remained unused for several months. During rehearsals at the house, however, "everybody was just milling around one afternoon when Pete Sears sat down at the piano in the living room and started to play a new song he had just written." Grace was in the kitchen making cracks about the bizarre health food milk shake John Barbata was whipping up. As Pete played in the other room, "it was like lightning had hit me in the head," she said. A moment later she appeared by the piano with her little black book. "I just happen to have some lyrics which fit with the verse, chorus and bridge—the whole thing," she said incredulously. "I could not believe it because you hardly ever get lyrics to fit music when both of them have been written independently." She and Pete were both excited about the song; they had the feeling of "doing something that was beautiful rather than merely making a moronic piece for the money-makers."

The album, released under the Oriental-sounding name *Dragonfly* on September 11, 1974, sold more than a million dollars' worth of records and earned them their first gold album since *Long John Silver* in 1972. The musicians were up from their first big hit. The vibes were positive. The communication was good but Grace could not have cared less. "I had not gone into rock and roll to make a fast buck," she said, "I did it to have fun," which was getting harder to get than the buck.

Though everybody was getting along in Starship, it was now a business. "And I didn't want to be there any more," Grace said quietly. Extrication was not so easy, however. "I kept thinking that I was going to be able to do it," she said, "even though I didn't like the way things were going. I kept telling myself that things were going to get better but a very real part of me already knew it was over."

In Phoenix, Arizona, as Grace was walking around the hotel pool to go to her room, she saw several guys in the crew, including Skip, looking at the girls at the next table. She sat down with them and listened to them trying to figure out what sort of clever remark would get them to come over and "get it on." Skip said: "Why don't you just be honest?" And with that, he turned his head in their direction and smiled: "I think you're good-looking —come over here!" Amazing, Grace thought; "the girls smiled and giggled and came over to join us for fifteen of the worst banana daiquiris ever concocted." At about five o'clock that afternoon Grace had to do an interview at one of the local radio stations with Craig. They asked Skip, who at this point was carrying around a bottle of champagne, to come along with them. "It was a good day, goofing around with the disc jockeys, cracking jokes and being *pleasantly* silly for a change." Grace and Skip spent the night together.

Paul did not catch on for months. "He was convinced that Skip was some kind of fruit. Since Paul did not want to go drinking or partying with me, he was glad that I finally had some friend to hang around the bars with," she said. "Paul would stay in the room smoking dope, watching television, writing songs and talking on the phone. At least that is what I assumed he was doing. He couldn't have brought too many women around since we had adjoining rooms. He was used to me being out at night with some of the guys in the group, either in the hotel bars or just hanging out in the rooms. It was no big deal. On the road those are two of the most convenient options we had."

At the age of thirty-six, Grace had finally found an alter ego in twenty-three-year-old Skip. "He's very much like I am in weakness and strength. As young as he is he taught me more about myself than anybody else. In other words, what I do, he feels."

Though everybody in the band knew, Paul was still unaware of the new situation. "He and Grace always had a free relationship," said Barbata. "She never really fucked around on him but they both had their own rooms and did their separate things." As things were getting heavy between Grace and Skip, the members of the band started getting nervous. "I was worried about the group breaking up if Grace and Paul split," said Barbata. "So I asked Paul what was going on. I told him that the two of them were more friendly than he thought."

Paul confronted Grace and asked her what was going on. "Our rooms were adjoining," said Barbata, "and I could hear them fighting. Then Grace came out on the balcony where I was looking out smoking a joint. She burst into tears. I tried to console her and tell her not to worry. I was pretty upset because things were going great and this could break up the band."

The incident triggered repressed hostilities. Behind closed doors Grace and Paul continued bickering. The handwriting was on the wall. In Virginia they started to fight about some small matter. "It built up," Grace said, "until I finally cried: 'Screw it. I'm going with Skip to Philadelphia.' I don't know why I said it. Skip hadn't even asked me to go to Philadelphia but I guess I was mad and sick of fighting." As the tensions reached a peak, she spilled the beans about the affair and marched out the door. "I headed down to the lounge because I had heard they had a five-foot television screen and I figured I might as well watch it until I cooled down."

About fifteen minutes later Paul stormed through the door. He grabbed her by the hair, caveman style, and dragged her along the floor to the stairs.

He shoved her into his room and picked up a gun. "He pushed me down on the floor and I figured I had better stay there. I didn't think he was going to kill me but I did think he was going to shoot the gun off," Grace said. The whole time they had kept up a running dialogue of abuses. Finally Paul picked up the phone and dialed Bill Thompson. "He told him to get here, before he did something stupid with this gun."

Thompson cooled Paul down for the moment, and Grace fled around the building to Skip's room on the other side of the corridor. "I told him Paul had a gun. Skip looked very calm, but he probably thought, how did I ever get involved with this asshole. But he just acted very pleasant under the circumstances."

The next night they performed a concert at William and Mary College. Grace's head was wracked with confusion. "I kept wondering what the hell I was doing to myself, Paul, China and Skip. I am with this man and we have a child—and a band. I can't just go hog-wild over this young kid because he is a good drinking buddy and I happen to like his sense of humor and looks. I figured I ought to take a second look at what I am doing here. I was beginning to think that I was acting like a jerk. I wasn't seventeen."

When the tour ended Skip went on the road with Stephen Stills. Grace went home with Paul and the band. "I spent the next couple of weeks trying to figure out for myself what I ought to do with this relationship. I sat in my room a lot thinking. Asking somebody else what I ought to do about my relationships is like asking somebody else if I am hungry. How can anybody with a different body and mind figure out what I want to do?"

The band, ironically, hit the peak as the personal relationship of Grace and Paul was hitting rock bottom. In February, they had gone into Wally Heider's to record the album *Red Octopus*, which knocked Elton John out of the first position on the *Billboard, Cashbox* and *Record World* charts. Over the next ten months, it sold two million copies, one of the biggest-selling albums of 1975. Its commercial impact far exceeded the sales of any album of the Airplane, even *Surrealistic Pillow*. Thompson was elated but Grace was growing more and more depressed.

The lyrics on *Dragonfly* had at least been a stab at thought-provoking statements; a rethinking of the values of the 1960s in a new context. Though Grace could live with this new direction and revision of the original perspective, "I did not like the way I could tell things were going." Marty had returned to the band tangentially. Paul had phoned him and Marty mentioned his new song "Caroline" as being a possibility for the album. It became the final cut on the first side of *Dragonfly*. A paean to wanderlust, it was the most popular and commercial song on the album, its sensibility having coincided with the growing trend in the industry away from social movements toward a broad-based romanticism which could be understood and enjoyed by a mass audience. "On *Red Octopus* there was this line which went something like—'Baby, if I had your love, I'd have everything.' Oh brother," Grace intoned, "this is like going back to being a senior in high school."

More than half of the songs on *Red Octopus* were just the same "pubescent bullshit," said Grace. "They did not say anything new nor did they have any unusual expression. Unless you have a unique way of expressing boy loves girl or girl loves boy, it's a waste of time. Paul Williams wrote a great love song in 'Evergreen' because the imagery had never been used—at least not in my memory. And Paul McCartney came right out in 'Silly Love Songs' and said that what he was doing was not unique—so it turned out to be unique saying it like that. Marty did it in 'Miracles.' That was a good song because the imagery was special, but what the rest of us were doing was sitting around writing songs without inspiration. I did it on *Red Octopus*. I wrote this song 'Al Garimasu' which basically says that love is love in all languages. I was trying to do the 'love-song/hot-record' routine without inspiration, and, consequently, without success.

"I saw during this period what was happening to us. I saw myself and the other people around me heading downhill for the dollar. I saw about half of the songs on that album were filled with the inanity that punctuates the repetition that happens when you are not writing out of your own perceptions but for the marketplace. And I did not want to do it."

On the first cut of *Red Octopus* in the song entitled "Fast Buck Freddie," she revealed her own antipathy to the whole deal. "It was like watching myself doing a free fall from an airplane, without a parachute. The ground was coming up fast, and it had dollar signs all over it."

Still, she never confronted Paul or Bill Thompson with her strong antipathy to the direction in which they were going. On the one hand, she was enjoying the money and the luxury of the riches surrounding her. On the other hand, it was becoming clearer and clearer that this was not the kind of life she wanted to lead. "But I wasn't sure what else was out there," she said, "and even if there was something better, I had no assurances that I would have the strength and luck to find it."

Skip had naturally been fired from the crew after the last go-round. "It was no big deal," said Grace. "It wasn't as if he was tied to *one* corporation. He wasn't working for IBM. He was still working with the lighting company in Philadelphia, so he just went out with the other bands, and we communicated by telephone for months. He came out to go to Pete Sears' wedding." During the ceremony, as she listened to Sears and his wife Jeanette exchange vows, "it touched me to hear what people start out thinking of each other, and then it hurt me to realize how fast, particularly in California, the ending of the love comes down."

Jeanette received a personal note from Grace, touching in its childlike sincerity, telling her how lucky she was to have found love. "I'm so stupid," Grace explained, "that at the age of thirty-six I still want to believe in the fantasy. I want to believe the relationship between a man and woman can always remain beautiful."

That night she went home to Paul; but a few days later, Jacky gave her a picture of Skip and her together at the wedding. Grace started to cry. "The more I talked to Skip, the more I realized that he was not just a drinking buddy. The closer I got to him, the more I liked him. I finally told Pat that I was going with Sally to Carmel to stay in the Hog's Breath Inn there, which was owned by Clint Eastwood, because Sally wanted to meet him."

In actuality, however, Sally and she took off for the airport. Sally, whose marriage to Spencer had ended, was interested in Stephen Stills now—and Skip was then touring with him. "We both decided to fly where they were—Anchorage, Alaska."

They got to the airport to learn that there was a strike. "We had to take five planes to get to Alaska," said Grace, "and then when we got to the hotel, none of the guys were around." Sally hooked up with Stills more or less but ended up with his keyboard player Jerry Aiello. Grace waited around her hotel room for Skip. Three or four hours later, he knocked. "When I opened the door, he was leaning against the wall in a fireman's helmet with flashing lights and sirens going off."

In June 1976, she had a long talk with Paul. "I told him I needed a tremendous amount of freedom," she said, "and he told me that I had it. He would give it to me. But that wasn't what I wanted. I couldn't live with that kind of setup. It was a schizoid life and too hypocritical for me. I couldn't go around carrying twenty pounds of guilt and splitting myself up into pieces like that. I told him that I was interested in Skip but even if things didn't work out with Skip, it wasn't fair to Paul or China if I was going to keep doing this kind of thing. I realized what I was doing might possibly be repeated again and again and that style of living would inevitably hurt all three of us."

Through want ads in the San Francisco *Chronicle* Grace found a small apartment for $350 a month in Sausalito. She furnished it in a week and moved her stuff in. Sally moved in for a while. China stayed a week with Grace, a week with Paul. "Finally I remember going for a ride with Paul to Twin Peaks when I said what I thought I should make clear to him." She told him that she was not moving back. "It was not easy but sometimes there are things you have to do that are immediately unpleasant but you just have a feeling, you just know it has to be that way."

Throughout this transition, she was drinking heavily with Sally. Skip could not stand watching her abuse herself in that way. "Finally he told me it was either the bottle or him," she said. "I told him goodbye and he walked out the door and went to the airport. An hour later he was back again. I guess he knew I loved him."

On the Starship's next tour she would sing in one town, then fly to the Stephen Stills tour to be with Skip for the day off. In the morning she would get on a plane, fly to the Starship tour and sing that night in concert. This went on every other day for two tours. She was in Chicago with Skip one night when he suddenly and quite seriously asked her to marry him. They had both been out drinking that evening, so she suggested that he ask her again in the morning when he was sober. The next morning when she woke up he had gone to work, but on the pillow there was a note. It was a sober proposal of marriage.

22

On November 29, 1976, Grace married Skip at the Royal Lahaina Hotel in Maui, Hawaii. Paul and Marty were not there but just about everybody else in the band flew over to the islands. "Those people who couldn't afford to go themselves went anyway," said Jacky. "Grace picked up the twenty-thousand-dollar bill. It was a first-class affair all the way. It was a small fortune but she spared no expense." China was flower girl. Virginia and Ivan Wing came. For her wedding gown Grace bought a white Hawaiian wedding dress "and two minutes before the ceremony my mother and I were still sewing organdy and silk flowers on it."

The ceremony was set outside on a terrace. "Both Skip and I loved to look at the Hawaiian sunsets." So, at around six-thirty, the bride and groom exchanged vows underneath a bank of flowers. "If we looked just past the flowers we could see the enormous glowing sky. The whole thing was like a soft fire, warm, colorful and happy."

Before moving out from Paul and China, Grace had had a heart-to-heart and very adult conversation with her five-year-old daughter. "I told her she was going to spend half her time with Paul and the other half with me," Grace said. "A lot of people say they stay together for the child, but I don't think it's healthy for a person to grow up in an atmosphere of strained companionship."

Though Skip was reinstated as lighting director of Starship, everybody was quietly hoping the guy would just go away and Grace would "go home" with Paul. "They were afraid that Skip was going to take me away from the band," she said. "They were afraid that he was going to turn me off to them and break up this good thing we had going."

The band continued to rack up platinum albums. Both *Spitfire* and *Earth* scored in the top 5 of the *Billboard* charts and justified RCA's investment in the band. Despite the money pouring in, the group was still being torn apart by internal dissension. Besides the schism between Paul and Grace, Marty had refused to sign a long-term contract with RCA or Grunt. He was working on an album-by-album basis, which gave him tremendous leverage in the band since he was bringing in the hit single material. He played it cool with the other musicians, showing up for rehearsals erratically and hanging up their plans to tour for over a year because he was doing other things.

Marty was perhaps entitled to the power trip as a retribution for his original loss of status after founding the Airplane, but he reclaimed his position with a vengeance. Grace was not immune to his vindication. After complaining about her background harmonies breaking up the structure of his songs for more than ten years, he decided to give her a dose of her own medicine. During one of her performances of her song entitled "Play on Love," he started singing loud and off-key background harmonies, which drove her to a mixture of outrage and tears in her dressing room. "Grace can really dish it out," he said, "but she sure can't take it."

Balin's vengeance was only one of similar plays which characterized the rapport of the band. "Pete Sears wasn't getting his artistic songs on the albums," Grace noted. "John Barbata wanted to play stadiums and pull in the bucks but Paul did not like the acoustics in the big halls." The Grunt office was sending her out on silly publicity stunts like cake-judging contests. "I was smiling and going along with it because we had to keep the publicity machine oiled while we were waiting for Marty to decide whether or not he was going to go on the road. I was sober for around a year," she said, "and I was just appalled by what I was seeing around me. I knew if I stuck around this scene much longer I'd not only need a psychiatrist but that psychiatrist would have to lock me up in a nuthouse."

Still, there was another record to make to maintain her contract with RCA, and her loyalty and love for Paul and China and a whole bag of guilt about letting down people with whom she had worked for fifteen years. In the spring of 1978 Jefferson Starship took off on their first tour in more than a year. Marty Balin had finally decided to go along. Though she didn't tell anybody, Grace was convinced that these were her final moments with the band. "I figured I would complete this tour and make one more album." When Mel Ilberman came to see the band in Boston, Grace looked radiant. She performed well. By the time she performed at the Nassau Coliseum in New York, however, she was acting kind of peculiar. She had withdrawn from the other members of the band and was sitting alone in the dressing room looking as though she was waiting for a bus rather than an evening of music. "I had driven somewhere with John Barbata and Bill Thompson," she said, "and heard Barbata telling Thompson that we should keep on playing these enormous things. He said, 'Let's go for the big money.'"

After two sold-out concerts for thousands of fourteen-year-olds at the Nassau Coliseum, Grace had had enough. "I was well aware that I had to leave. I couldn't make it to the end." Still, she persevered. "I was hoping to make it through the European tour." On the train in Germany, however, she started throwing up and running to the bathroom. At the hotel in Lorelei, the doctor told her that she was very sick and could not play the concert that evening. "Even if he had given me a clean bill of health," she said, "I still couldn't have gone on. I was going to the bathroom and throwing up every ten minutes. Nobody wants to pay money to see that on stage."

Skip went to tell Thompson that Grace could not go on. Thompson called a meeting of the band in Grace's room which turned into a catharsis. "It was an incredible avalanche of stuff," she said, "and I finally had to face up. I told them I couldn't keep imitating myself, the smart-aleck acid tongue of the sixties. We had all changed in different directions, and I couldn't continue doing the current style, which was M-O-R, aiming for money. The material was not new or interesting. Everybody was just waiting for Marty to bring in another hit like 'Miracles.' Our sound equipment was so big nobody including our sound men knew how to run it. The friction between Paul and Skip was splitting me down the middle.

"I told them I was making my exit now before they had to put me in a nuthouse. I told them I wanted to know myself and handle myself. I wanted to be able to change instead of perpetuating this lunatic I had created named Grace Slick."

Marty applauded her soliloquy. "He told me that he was glad I had finally done it." Paul could not accept her decision. "He just couldn't believe things were that bad. He kept asking me what was wrong and suggesting that instead of leaving why didn't I just stick around and try to change what it was I didn't like.

"I told him that you can't change fifty grown people's personalities. You can't change anybody but yourself. I didn't want to run him or play Miss Hotstuff and tell everybody how to act. That's dictator time. What I wanted to do is what this person Grace has to do or needs to do in order to grow."

The band thought it would make some sense to play the concert doing Marty's material but Paul wouldn't do it. When the promoter got up on stage to announce the Starship would not perform that evening but would play free at a future date, the audience went crazy. They started throwing beer bottles and yelling obscenities. By the next morning when Grace and Skip drove out to the site the audience had burned down everything on the stage and ravaged the premises. "The guitars, the drums, the sound equipment were ashes," said Grace, who climbed on the only amp left at the side of the stage which had not been set on fire. "I felt that the ashes marked the end of a fifteen-year cycle," she said. "It was all kind of weird but as I sat there I had a strong feeling that we had all just survived our own deaths."

Rising slowly she walked down the dirt road away from the wreckage. "I could think of the fire as either the destroyer or cleanser. I didn't say a word to Skip. We just looked at each other.

"I knew the next section of my life was going to be quite

different from the last one. What I would like to do from there on was not exactly clear. I knew I had choices to make and that some of them would affect the immediate future of quite a few people. But we have all been survivors so far and that fact in itself means there is much more to be done. There is a spirit of love that can be ignored or cherished, and I didn't want to experience the results of ignorance again if I could possibly help it. That would mean a 180-degree change of attitudes and objectives. If I was willing to open up and let the unknown become familiar, the possibilities for the future were endless."